Contents

Sound System

The Political Power of Music

Dave Randall

PlutoPress
www.plutobooks.com

First published 2017 by Pluto Press
345 Archway Road, London N6 5AA

www.plutobooks.com

The Left Book Club, founded in 2014, company number 9338285
pays homage to the original Left Book Club founded by Victor Gollancz
in 1936.

British Library Cataloguing in Publication Data
A catalogue record for this book is available from the British Library

ISBN   978 0 7453 9930 0   Paperback
ISBN   978 1 7868 0034 3   PDF eBook
ISBN   978 1 7868 0036 7   Kindle eBook
ISBN   978 1 7868 0035 0   EPUB eBook

This book is printed on paper suitable for recycling and made from fully
managed and sustained forest sources. Logging, pulping and manufacturing
processes are expected to conform to the environmental standards of the
country of origin.

Typeset by Stanford DTP Services, Northampton, England

Simultaneously printed in the United Kingdom and United States of America

For Lucy Angell John

Series Preface

The first Left Book Club (1936–48) had 57,000 members, had distributed two million books, and had formed 1,200 workplace and local groups by the time it peaked in 1939. LBC members were active throughout the labour and radical movement at the time, and the Club became an educational mass movement, remodelling British public opinion and contributing substantially to the Labour landslide of 1945 and the construction of the welfare state.

Publisher Victor Gollancz, the driving force, saw the LBC as a movement against poverty, fascism, and the growing threat of war. He aimed to resist the tide of austerity and appeasement, and to present radical ideas for progressive social change in the interests of working people. The Club was about enlightenment, empowerment, and collective organisation.

The world today faces a crisis on the scale of the 1930s. Capitalism is trapped in a long-term crisis. Financialisation and austerity are shrinking demand, deepening the depression, and widening social inequalities. The social fabric is being torn apart. International relations are increasingly tense and militarised. War threatens on several fronts, while fascist and racist organisations are gaining ground across much of Europe. Global warming threatens the planet and the whole of humanity with climate catastrophe. Workplace organisation has been weakened, and social democratic parties have been hollowed out by acceptance of pro-market dogma. Society has become more atomised, and mainstream politics suffers an acute democratic deficit.

Yet the last decade has seen historically unprecedented levels of participation in street protest, implying a mass audience for progressive alternatives. But socialist ideas are no longer, as in the immediate post-war period, 'in the tea'. One of neoliberalism's achievements has been to undermine ideas of solidarity, collective provision, and public service.

The Left Book Club aspires to meet this ideological challenge. Our aim is to offer high-quality books at affordable prices that are carefully selected to address the central issues of the day and to be accessible to a wide general audience. Our list represents the full range of progressive traditions, perspectives, and ideas. We hope the books will be used as the basis of reading circles, discussion groups, and other educational and cultural activities relevant to developing, sharing, and disseminating ideas for change in the interests of the common people at home and abroad.

The Left Book Club collective

Acknowledgements

This short book had a long gestation. It is the culmination of countless conversations and other moments shared with good people too numerous to list. I'm indebted to you all. There are, of course, a few who must be mentioned by name. Let me begin with my brilliant editor David Castle, who somehow saw potential in my scattered notes from the start and patiently steered them in the required direction. Thanks also to Emily, Melanie, Kieran, Neda, Robert, Simon, Chris and all the other gifted members of the Pluto Press team. It's a pleasure to work with you. It's also a privilege to be published as part of the Left Book Club, which is an excellent initiative. My gratitude to Jonathan Maunder who first introduced me to Pluto Press and whose enthusiasm for the book encouraged me immensely. A number of friends have provided invaluable feedback and advice. Chris Nineham, Gareth Mason, Carol Robinson, Tony Horner and Robin Gibson were all kind enough to cast their expert eyes over early drafts. I owe you all several pints of Brixton's finest.

Some of the content was 'road-tested' at a series of events called 'The Rest is Noise: Brixton', which I organised after being inspired by the South Bank festival of a similar name. Thanks to Alex Ross, author of *The*

Rest is Noise, for giving the series his blessing, and Jude Kelly for encouraging me when I first proposed the idea – and for her ongoing support. Also to Gillian Moore who spoke at the first event and all the other contributors – among them Dominic Murcott, Susanna Eastburn, Denys Baptiste, Colin Wilson, Estelle Cooch, Simon Behrman, Anindya Bhattacharyya and Heidi Heidelberg. Thanks to David Byrne for kindly lending me his copy of Cornelius Cardew's *Stockhausen Serves Imperialism*. I must also acknowledge my debt to the great Italian Marxist Antonio Gramsci. He isn't mentioned in the book, but his ideas inform some of its key themes. Many friends, in different ways, have encouraged and helped me: Kai Brown, Sudha Kheterpal, Chris Sly, Alix Wilding, Simon Mylius, Jamie Catto, Yasmin Khan, Andy Marlow, Tania Matos, Steve Jones, Rob Owen, Mark Bergfeld, John Rees, Sylvia Ferreira, Ben Windsor, Emma Quinn, Andy Richardson, Jenny Adejayan, Chipo Chung, Pete Miser, Shingai Shoniwa, Tom Robinson, Bobby Whiskers, Steve Hack, Henna Malik, Andy Sankey, Mark Bergin and Alex Forster to name a few. Thanks also to Jamilla and the Afrane family for looking after me in Ghana and Ann-Marie and all my Trinidadian family for such a memorable time in Port of Spain.

I'd like to give a loving shout-out to all the musicians I've had the privilege of working with over the course of my career so far. Special mention to the members of Slovo, Faithless, 1 Giant Leap, Sleeping In Vilna,

Emiliana Torrini, Sinead O'Connor, Roland Gift, Doudou Cissoko, Jean-Jacques Plante, Fausat Abioye and all 'The Happening' musicians. Also Rita Ray and Max Reinhardt of the wondrous Mwalimu Express, Raye Cosbert of Metropolis Music, Paul Bolton of X-ray Touring, Herman Verkade of Brixtown Records and Sean McLoughlin and Colette Bailey of Metal. Big hugs to the other artists, choreographers and filmmakers I've had the pleasure of collaborating with – in particular Feeding The Fish, Ahmed Masoud and Al-Zaytouna, and my partner in Pac-woman, popcorn and Brooklyn beers: the fearless, tireless and über-talented Jen Marlowe. To my lovely mum and dad . . . thank you for everything. Finally, and most importantly, endless love and gratitude to my amazing partner Lucy Angell John. This one's for you!

CHAPTER ONE

Roots

Look around any crowded street, bus or subway carriage almost anywhere in the world and you see people experiencing music. It spills from a sea of headphones and reverberates from shops, cars, buskers, bars, places of worship and homes. Our lives are steeped in the stuff. It lulls us to sleep when we are babies and helps us acquire language. It's part of children's play and expresses our identity as we navigate our way into adulthood. It walks us down the aisle and marches us off to war. To paraphrase Quincy Jones, it is the 'emotion lotion' applied to adverts and films. It can help create the atmosphere in which we seduce our lovers, make babies and reminisce when we are old. Finally, it plays tinnily from the speakers of crematoriums as we slip behind the final curtain.

For me, music is also a job. I'm writing these words from seat 27H of an American Airlines Boeing 777, 36,000 feet above the Atlantic. My current boss, the Irish singer Sinead O'Connor, sits a few rows ahead in business class. We, along with the rest of her new band, are flying to Los Angeles, where we are due to perform in a couple of days. I've been lucky in my career. Getting the call to play guitar for Sinead was the latest piece of good fortune. Over the past 20 years, I've toured four continents and countless countries with some amazing artists. I've seen people, places and events that an ordinary Essex boy like me would never have otherwise seen. Before I joined the group Faithless back in 1996, I'd hardly left the country. There are downsides. More late nights, long flights and free booze than any doctor would recommend and a creeping sense of financial insecurity, occasionally abated by a big tour, though never for long. But questions of health and wealth are not those that spin around my head like old shellac 78s. As I sit wakeful on this long-haul my thoughts settle on questions of music. There is no doubt that music matters to people, but what is its impact on society? How does this universal human activity reflect changes in economics, technology and politics? How has music shaped our world – and what contribution can it make to the struggle for a better one?

My political awakening began when I was a teenager. I'd grown up in the 1980s in a seaside town known for spiteful proto-punk rhythm & blues and a very long pier (1.34 miles). Local musicians like to describe our area as the 'Thames delta'. I somehow rose from the coveted position of 'Saturday boy' in the local guitar shop to roadie for blues-rock heroes the Hamsters. My world became the backseat of a splitter van, pubs, bikers' clubs and late night truck stops across the UK. Politics may well have remained largely off my radar, were it not for one August night spent in a field in Northamptonshire. Some mates had invited me to a music festival called Greenbelt, run by left-wing Christians. In a packed marquee between bands, the DJ dropped a tune by the Special AKA: 'Free Nelson Mandela'. I had no idea who Nelson Mandela was, but I knew by the end of the first chorus I wanted him to be free. In that moment, surrounded by thousands of festival goers hollering the hook, I learned – instinctively felt – that the future is unwritten and ordinary people like me could have a say. Music, I realised, is our weapon.

In 1996 I got my first real break. After playing for a string of semi-professional bands I was finally offered a fulltime gig. Faithless had started as a studio project assembled by the ambitious dance music producer Rollo Armstrong. With their tune 'Insomnia' racing up charts across Europe demands for a tour started to flood in from label managers convinced that a 'proper' live band would secure sales and longevity in a way DJ sets alone would not. I was one lucky beneficiary of this foresight. Until then I'd been content squeezing into old splitter vans, but now my lift took the form of luxury tour buses and aeroplanes.

Being a part of a band when it breaks onto the international circuit is exhilarating. I don't think anyone considered, in those early days, the possibility that Faithless would go on to become one of the biggest dance music acts in recent history – or that our occasional singer Dido would one day sell over 30 million albums in her own right. Back then just being on a tour bus, flying to a gig and having a crew were thrilling signs that we'd 'made it'. One of the first things to learn was the language of touring. Europe hadn't yet agreed to monetary union, so every day meant a different currency. All were labelled 'shitters', as in: 'have you got any shitters?' Distances were measured in 'clicks', fans were 'punters', gaffa tape found stuck to the sole of your shoe 'gig turds' and bottle openers 'gig spanners'. Tour bus rules included sleeping with your feet facing forward (less likely to break your neck in the event of a crash) and no pooing in the toilet (pees only). If during a night-time gas-stop you get off the bus to find a toilet, make sure you tell the driver. Our percussionist learned that lesson the hard way. Wearing only boxer shorts and a T-shirt, he emerged from a petrol station restroom somewhere in Germany to see the tour bus disappearing into the distance. It wasn't until the soundcheck, some twelve hours and two national borders later that we realised he was missing. The crew guys – and on that first tour they were all male – seemed to be seasoned sages of the road. They were lovable, sometimes scary, often hilarious, and by far the hardest working and hardest drinking of all the music professionals (I hadn't yet met any riggers). One of their mantras, repeated with dry irony, was 'Hurry Up . . . And Wait'. There's a LOT of waiting around.

'Free Nelson Mandela' had planted a seed in my mind. Soon after I heard it, other artists caught my ear. Billy Bragg, Public Enemy, the Disposable Heroes of Hiphoprisy, Ani DiFranco and Rage Against The Machine all underlined the idea that music could be a political force in the world. Now I was part of an up-and-coming band, I wanted to know more about this strange power. I decided to use all that waiting around time to read about the politics of pop.

CHAPTER TWO

Culture

Jukebox Suckers

I soon discovered the relationship between music and politics has been contemplated for quite some time. In 380 BC, Plato noted Socrates' warning that 'a change to a new type of music is something to beware of as a hazard of all our fortunes. For the modes of music are never disturbed without unsettling of the most fundamental political and social conventions'.[1] The emperors of China set up an Imperial Music Bureau tasked with supervising court music and keeping an ear on the music of the masses, believing it to be a telling portent of social unrest. Music was also deployed by both sides during Europe's reformation and the hundred years of state sponsored terror that followed. The Catholic Church even set up a *Vatican's Got Talent*-style panel of cardinals at the Council of Trent in the mid-1500s, to judge which composer could best deliver them a musical knock-out (Giovanni Pierluigi da Palestrina got the gig).

In the modern era, a German intellectual called Theodor Adorno ruminated on the subject, writing his most important essays in the 1940s. Sociologist and Mercury Music Prize impresario Simon Frith considered Adorno's to be 'the most systematic and the most searing analysis of mass culture and the most challenging for anyone claiming a scrap of value for the products that come churning out of the music industry'.[2] Adorno was certainly prolific. He wrote around a million words about music and also found time to train as a classical pianist. He particularly admired the ground-breaking Austrian composer Arnold Schoenberg and studied composition for three years with Schoenberg's one-time student, Alban Berg. Adorno's devotion to challenging new European music was undeniable, but as Frith implies, he didn't like pop.

Adorno was part of a group of left-leaning scholars known as the Frankfurt School. The rise of the Nazis forced the school to relocate to New York City in 1935. Although the USA provided Adorno with refuge from the Nazis, he didn't see it as 'the land of the free'. Instead he insisted that it had more in common with Nazi Germany and Stalin's Russia than people realised. It too was based on an economic system that gave a monopoly of power to the few. Focusing on the output of America's original hit factory – a New York street filled with songwriters and publishers nicknamed 'Tin Pan Alley' – Adorno delivered his damning assessment. Like tins of baked beans or any other mass manufactured commodity, pop hits, he noted, were pumped out by the production lines of a cynical 'Culture Industry' to standardised formulae. Sure, the melodies change a little from song to song, but only to give a fake impression of originality and authenticity. Lapped up by a mass audience who knew no better, this was music designed to blunt our desire to think for ourselves. As David Byrne puts it:

Adorno saw the jukebox as a machine that drew 'suckers' into pubs with the promise of joy and happiness. But, like a drug, instead of bringing real happiness, the music heard on jukeboxes only creates more desire for itself. He might be right, but he might also have been someone who never had a good time in a honky-tonk.[3]

Adorno never really differentiated between mainstream commercial pop and other less formulaic popular sounds. Had he taken time to appreciate the varied and often anti-establishment popular music made beyond Tin Pan Alley, he may have arrived at a more nuanced view. That he didn't is surprising – there was certainly plenty of it. During the inter-war Weimar Republic of Adorno's native Germany, Kurt Weill and Bertolt Brecht brought socialist opera to the masses with an adaptation of John Gay's *Beggar's Opera* entitled *Threepenny Opera* (its songs would later be covered by artists as diverse as Ella Fitzgerald, Michael Bublé, Pet Shop Boys and Tom

Waits). Others explored social questions and celebrated sexual diversity through the decadent Berlin cabaret scene. Meanwhile, in the US, a coalition of left-wing intellectuals, including the influential folklorist Alan Lomax, decided popular culture provided an important platform for politics. They championed folk and blues musicians including Woody Guthrie and Lead Belly and argued that African American musical traditions such as New Orleans Jazz were a form of 'proletarian protest and pride'. None of this seemed to permeate Adorno's world, or at least influence his position. He remained steadfast in his belief that progress was found only in serious music such as Schoenberg's – music that dismantled traditional approaches to harmony and replaced them with new sounds to stimulate the intellect as well as stir the soul: 'It requires the listener spontaneously to compose its inner movements and demands of him not mere contemplation but *praxis*.'[4]

In his later years Adorno did concede that there was some value to what he called 'low-brow' art: 'The distinction between entertainment and autonomous art points to a qualitative difference that ought to be retained, provided one does not overlook the hollowness of the concept of serious art or the validity of unregimented impulses in low-brow art.'[5] But his views remained fundamentally the same as those he articulated in the 1940s. Pop can only strengthen the hand of the powers that be: 'Even the best-intentioned reformers who use an impoverished and debased language to recommend renewal, strengthen the very power of the established order they are trying to break.'[6]

Seemingly on the opposite side to Adorno is a branch of cultural theory that celebrates everything pop in all its kitsch, consumerist glory. As well as throwing out the hierarchy implicit in Adorno's conclusions (difficult art music good, pop music bad), its advocates also rejected the narrow focus of musicology. They weren't just concerned with the sound and structure of the music itself – they were also interested in the messages communicated through fashion choices, record covers, promo shots and all the other tools of music marketing. By the late 1970s, the approach had become an established part of a new field called Cultural Studies. Thinking seriously about pop was acceptable – trendy even. But there's no doubt snobbery persisted. Some intellectuals simply indulged their fascination with the exotic proletariat and their strange ways. As keen ornithologists might, sociologists discussed the amusing mating rituals and colourful plumage of the working class. But others started from a position of solidarity. Marxists including Stuart Hall and Dick Hebdige saw symbolic political resistance and class pride in youth cultures. To identify as a 'teddy boy', 'mod', 'rocker', 'skinhead', 'punk', or whatever, was to reclaim some control over your life – to actively choose your identity. Music that went with that identity therefore, was nothing less than the soundtrack of class struggle. With this belief, the left-leaning cultural theorists joined a long tradition of progressives who have championed folk and popular music, believing that since the ruling class have their much revered 'high' culture, we should celebrate our own 'popular' culture.

So, on the one hand we have Adorno who sees popular music as a sinister weapon of mass distraction. On the other, the various champions of popular culture who encourage us to celebrate popular music, with all its marketing trinkets and charms, as a true voice of the people.

To complicate matters further, there emerged in the 1950s and '60s another group of left-leaning music lovers who dealt with the apparent dilemma by rejecting both high-brow 'serious' music *and* commercial pop. They included a group of musicians based at Morley College, south London, who coalesced around the British composer Cornelius Cardew. Schoenberg and similar composers, they decided, were too formal in their approach to music, too technically difficult, and therefore elitist. Commercial pop was too dumbed down, mass manufactured and corporate. Music, they argued, should be freer in form and more open in terms of who could participate. They decided to create an orchestra with a largely improvised repertoire and welcomed into its ranks classically trained players, musicians from other traditions and non-musicians. The result was the Scratch Orchestra formed in 1969. As one of its members described: 'What bound together the varied membership of the Scratch Orchestra [was] a common experience of the two oppressive blocs in our social and cultural environment – the "serious" music and art of the establishment on the one hand, and the commercialism of pop etc. on the other.'[7]

It seems to me that all the perspectives offer something useful. They help us to ask the right questions – to expand what we talk about when we talk about music. Adorno forces us to consider the possibility that music manufactured by a murky corporate industry may be an obstacle to our liberation. If you compare the tumbleweed turnout for most trade union elections with the media ballyhoo surrounding talent shows and celebrity gossip, Adorno's ideas start to make sense. We're encouraged to care more about who wins *The Voice* than how we can make our own voices heard. On the other hand, the pop-loving cultural theorists remind us that political messages can be conveyed through every artistic choice – even a haircut. State censors around the world would agree – many have banned songs, artwork, music videos and some have even forcibly shaven the heads of musicians or fans whose image they considered subversive. And the Scratch Orchestra, as well as the various improvising musicians who followed similar creative paths, encourage us to broaden our idea of what it means to be a musician, how music should be made and how it might sound. That's important in a world where far too many people are denied the pleasure of making music because they're intimidated by how specialised that skill seems to be. Too many of us think we're 'tone deaf' and have never been encouraged to let go of our inhibitions and join in.

But despite their contributions, I think the premise of all three positions is problematic. They all start with the assumption that the social impact of music is determined by *style* – how it's made and how it sounds. Then they ask us to pick a side: either 'classical', 'popular' or 'free improvised'. But are the styles really so separate? A quick flick through any serious history of music shows that for centuries folk and popular forms have influenced classical (or 'art') music and vice versa. The categories have always been more fluid than many of us think. Does it really make sense to accept the idea that 'high art' is 'theirs' and 'popular culture' is 'ours' – or the other way around? Should we really reject both in favour of a musical experiment – egalitarian in form but inaccessible for many listeners? The Scratch Orchestra wanted to change people's conceptions, but rarely in the early years did their audience outnumber them. They survived on Arts Council grants and refused to 'make concessions to the public'. It seems that elitism isn't only achieved by having a formal approach and tricky score. As orchestra member Rod Eley later acknowledged:

'It was the stock reaction of the alienated, bourgeois artist – withdrawal from social responsibility – 'art for art's sake'. At its worst the roots of the ambitions of the Orchestra lay in the Romantic pretension, expressed by Keats: 'All art aspires to the condition of music'. Music being a 'pure experience', untainted by mundane human or social concerns... No one yet understood that both these oppressive blocs – bourgeois establishment culture and pop commercialism – were only two facets of one world-wide system of oppression: the capitalist system.'[8]

I'd put it another way: no genre acts exclusively as a weapon of mass distraction and no genre is automatically and always on the side of progress. All forms of music can be used as part of a system of oppression, but they can also be part of the story of our liberation – the social meaning isn't fixed. In fact, the same piece of music or musical act can simultaneously have different meanings – some good, some not so good. This was something I learned in 1997 when Faithless were invited to tour Mandela's South Africa. I saw the tour as a gesture of solidarity and celebration – a multiracial band visiting the long boycotted and newly liberated rainbow nation. I've no doubt many of our fans interpreted it in the same way. But when, at a welcoming dinner organised by the promoter, I asked the young woman sitting next to me what her job was, she replied quite candidly and with a sweet smile, 'To get 18–25-year-olds to smoke'. It turned out that the tour was very visibly sponsored by Camel cigarettes. So far as our sponsors were concerned, our role was as Trojan horse for a new round of health damaging corporate exploitation in the troubled nation.

What has become clear to me is that the meaning of all music is *contested*. Style matters, but it doesn't have the final say. Even when the composer's intentions are clearly expressed, if music is heard in a particular context, its meaning can be hijacked for another cause. Take the example of acoustic folk – long associated with campfires, hobos, hippies and protest. Some fans in the 1960s were so convinced of the indivisibility of progressive politics and acoustic guitars that when Bob Dylan traded his for a Stratocaster at the 1965 Newport Folk Festival, he was booed by a section of the audience who considered the (musical) decision to be a (political) sell-out. Now you are more likely to hear acoustic folk on a corporate advert than a picket line. Those same associations are deployed by advertisers to bring brands a reassuring homespun, nostalgic, eco- and family-friendly charm. The classical avant-garde is also sometimes used in similarly cynical ways. Conversely, in the right circumstances, a disposable pop song might bring strength to those in the midst of revolution. The ballad 'E Depois do Adeus' (And after the farewell) started life as Portugal's entry for the Eurovision Song Contest in 1974. It scored a dismal three points and finished joint last. But later that year the song was chosen to signal the start of the 'Carnation Revolution' – a mass uprising that successfully ousted the dictator Marcello Caetano. Italy's Eurovision entry that year also caused political controversy, again due to its particular historical context. Entitled 'Si' (Yes), the Italian government became convinced it was an attempt at subliminal propaganda ahead of an intensely fought referendum on divorce. They resolved not to broadcast the competition. 'Si' did rather better than 'E Depois do Adeus'. It was only pipped to the top spot by Abba's 'Waterloo'. Seemingly innocuous pop songs can also accrue an aura of terror in times of turbulent upheaval. When Uganda's former President Idi Amin was tightening his grip on power, the state radio station played 'My Boy Lollipop' all day long, interspersing its sugary refrains with military men's threats and warnings of curfews. Writer Yasmin Alibhai-Brown, who experienced the coup and its brutal aftermath, told me that to this day she is unable to listen to the song.

The Beatles, the Kremlin and the CIA

The teenage me who saw music as a weapon was right. But it's one that can be seized by any side in a conflict. And the same piece of music or musical act can simulta-neously advance different agendas. Culture is contested and context is key.

To get a grasp on the complexities of this contest for culture's meaning it's helpful to look at some examples. Let's begin with the world's best known band and the era they dominated. The first of our Beatles tales reveals that even when rulers consciously create a context in which culture is seen to be supporting their values, simple tricks can sometimes subvert things. A few well-chosen words from John Lennon did just that one evening in 1963.

The Royal Variety Performance is an annual variety show usually held at the London Palladium and broadcast around the world. Jugglers, magicians, acrobats, singers and dancers vie to impress the well-heeled audience, their finishing flourishes followed by neat bows and crisp curtseys in the direction of the royal box. Originally called Royal Command Performances, the events have long helped to reinforce the notion that the whole of British society, including its most popular stars, know their place in the class hierarchy and are happy to be subjects of the Queen. This is popular culture placed in the frontline of a battle to reinforce ruling class values. Lennon was smart enough to see this and decided to get a shot off for the other side. Introducing the last song of the Beatles' set, he said to the audience, including the Queen Mother: 'For our last number I'd like to ask your help . . . Will the people in the cheaper seats clap your hands? And the rest of you – if you'll just rattle your jewellery.' It wasn't the first time a musician had made a class-conscious quip in public. The operas of Mozart and Verdi are full of depictions of the bad behaviour and hypocrisy of the nobility. What was ground-breaking was that the spectacle of a working-class lad making the rich squirm for a delicious moment had been beamed live into homes across Britain. Thanks to Lennon, an event organisers had intended as a display of polite deference had delivered the nation's first synchronised seditious smirk. Lennon had, jujitsu style, used the strength of the establishment – its ability to capture the attention of the nation with a state broadcast – against itself. He had dared to deploy the power of the Culture Industry, albeit in a very limited way, against the class who own it.

Meanwhile, unbeknown to the band, the Beatles were also becoming icons of rebellion behind the Iron Curtain. The Stalinist regimes tried to keep a strict control on popular culture and viewed Western pop with suspicion. Accordions and folk dances were officially sanctioned but rock and roll remained firmly off limits. Russian music journalist Artemy Troitsky described the scene: 'Being a young radical man I just hated all this, because it was all totally square, totally uncool; all the singers had the wrong haircuts, they were dressed like office clerks and they sang like Brezhnev at the Communist Party congress. Soviet culture was totally un-sexy.'[9]

Frustrated music lovers were desperate to get their hands on the latest releases from the West – in particular anything by the Beatles. In the mid-1960s they found a secret weapon in the form of roadside recording booths intended for homesick soldiers to record messages for their mums. Late at night, bootleggers would turn up with tapes of Beatles songs illicitly recorded from Radio Luxembourg and X-ray prints collected from the bins of hospital radiography departments, which served as makeshift vinyl. As Leslie Woodhead described: 'A black-market mushroomed fed by "records on ribs". Kids could listen to "I Feel Fine" on Uncle Sergei's lungs.' Rock and roll 'flexies' as they were known were hidden up sleeves and traded in dark alleys for three roubles a piece. Despite the dangers it posed to buyers and sellers, the Beatles virus raced across the Soviet empire. By the late 1960s, compact cassette tape players had arrived, enabling the mass bootlegging of the contraband 'records on ribs'. Beatle-mania soared. According to Troitsky, the band's impact can hardly be overstated: 'The "big bad" West had huge institutions which spent tens of millions of dollars [trying to] undermine the Soviet system. I'm sure that the impact of all those stupid Cold War institutions has been much, much smaller than the impact of the Beatles.'[10]

The story of the Beatles in the USSR reveals how music can become both subject and symbol of political rebellion for ordinary fans. The precise way the longhaired Liverpudlians were interpreted behind the Iron Curtain would have depended, among other things, on the perspective of the fan. For some of those subjected to the Soviet system, the band confirmed that life was better in the

West. Others felt they were engaged in a common struggle alongside the Fab Four against the corrupt values of older generations on both sides of the Cold War divide. Certainly the band was an annoyance for the Kremlin but not necessarily to the benefit of Washington.

What we do know is that Washington believed in the propaganda value of culture. During the height of the Cold War, millions of dollars were ploughed into CIA front organisations tasked with waging a cultural war. This little known chapter in Cold War realpolitik underlines just how significant states consider the potential power of culture to be. The centrepiece of the covert campaign was the Congress for Cultural Freedom, run by CIA agent Michael Josselson from 1950 to 1965. Its mission was to promote culture and provide creative opportunities that would help guide the intelligentsia of Western Europe away from the influence of Marxism towards a worldview more 'accommodating to the American way'. As Francis Stonor Saunders describes: 'Whether they liked it or not, whether they knew it or not, there were few writers, poets, artists, historians, scientists or critics in postwar Europe whose names are not in some way linked to this covert enterprise.'[11]

Musicians also played their part. Indeed, Josselson's 'Information Control Division' had its own music section presided over by the White Russian émigré composer Nicolas Nabokov. Ostensibly, his task was to oversee the purging of Nazis from German music, but the real priority was to build up a symbolic cultural bulwark against the Soviet Union. Nabokov turned a blind eye to the former crimes of even quite high profile Nazis if it helped the West to gain the upper hand in the cultural cold war. One example was Elizabeth Schwarzkopf – a singer and Nazi party member who had given concerts for the Waffen SS. She was described by Goebbels as 'blessed by God' after she took starring roles in his propaganda films. In the postwar years, following clearance by the Allied Control Commission, her career soared. She was later made a Dame of the British Empire.

Stalin also engaged in the cultural war. Sensing an opportunity to out-manoeuvre his opponents, he agreed to send an all-star delegation to the 'Cultural and Scientific Conference for World Peace' hosted at New York's Waldorf hotel in March 1949. Delegates had to push their way past right-wing pickets, furious that a platform had been given to the 'Commies', and lines of nuns sent to pray for the souls of participants deranged by 'Satanic seduction'. Playwright Arthur Miller, who had been invited to chair one of the conference debates, explained his decision to attend: 'For me . . . the conference was an effort to continue a good tradition that was presently menaced . . . the sharp post-war turn against the Soviets and in favour of a Germany unpurged of Nazis not only seemed ignoble but threatened another war that might indeed destroy Russia but bring down our own democracy as well.'[12]

CIA composer-in-chief Nicolas Nabokov had a different agenda – to skewer the reluctant star of the Soviet delegation, the acclaimed composer Dimitri Shostakovich. Nabokov made his way to a panel discussion at which Shostakovich was speaking and was finally called to take the floor:

[On such-and-such a date in No. X] of *Pravda* appeared an unsigned article that had all the looks of an editorial. It concerned three western composers: Paul Hindemith, Arnold Schoenberg, and Igor Stravinsky. In this article, they were branded, all three of them, as 'obscurantists', 'decadent bourgeois formalists' and 'lackeys of imperialist capitalism'. The performance of their music should 'therefore be prohibited in the USSR'. Does Mr Shostakovich personally agree with this official view as printed in Pravda?[13]

'*Provokatsya!*' (Provocation!), cried Russian delegates as KGB stooges hastily whispered instructions to an ashen-faced Shostakovich. Slowly the composer rose to his feet, head lowered, and murmured in Russian, 'I fully agree with this official view as printed in *Pravda*'.

It's interesting that one of the 'lackeys of imperialist capitalism' mentioned in the *Pravda* piece was Adorno's favourite, Arnold Schoenberg. The composer had led the way in new atonal sounds including an approach to composition known as 'twelve-tone technique' or 'serialism'. At its strictest, it stipulates that all twelve notes of the chromatic scale be used before any are repeated. The method helped composers to break away from traditional approaches to harmony which some felt imprisoned music in a world of hackneyed formulae and cliché. For fans such as Adorno the resulting unsettling sounds eloquently expressed the contradictions and tensions of the times. Perhaps Stalin disliked the music for the same reason – he wanted listeners in the USSR to be reminded of social harmony, progress, national pride and the triumph of 'socialism in one country' – not stirred by eerie dissonance. Nabokov sensed an opportunity. Since Stalin had proscribed the difficult new music, the West, he decided, should be seen to be actively celebrating it. This would demonstrate to the world the West's commitment to artistic freedom. He planned a music festival billed as a 'confident look into the future' – The International Conference of Twentieth Century Music. It was to take place in Rome in April 1954. Nabokov sent the first invitation to Igor Stravinsky who agreed to head up the festival's music advisory board. Twelve new composers (all influenced to some degree by serialism) would, it was decided, compete for a prize, with the winner picked by a special jury. It was, if you will, a sort of highbrow, Cold War, dodecaphonic *Pop Idol*. Although the competitors believed their compositions were helping to free music from the old laws of 'music's inner logic', it's a moot point as to how many ordinary music lovers equated their creations with liberty and progress. Pierre Boulez, himself a devotee of the outer edges of musical experimentation, thought the competition missed the point and shoehorned the new music into a bizarre modernist cul-de-sac. In a furious letter, he declared that Nabokov and his jurors knew nothing of the creative process and accused them of encouraging mediocrity. He concluded that the Congress' next venture should be in better taste, offering the suggestion of a conference on 'the role of the condom in the Twentieth century'.

However righteous was Boulez's rage, the American cultural cold warriors had bigger concerns than Nabokov's musical choices. The Achilles' heel in their propaganda campaign was the treatment of black people in the USA. In 1946 US Secretary of State James Byrnes attempted to protest the Soviet denial of voting rights in the Balkans only to be reminded by the Soviets that 'The Negroes of Mr Byrnes' own state of South Carolina were denied the same right'. Again it was culture that CIA psychological warfare experts turned to in their attempt to improve the international image of race relations in the US. They established a secret Cultural Presentation Committee tasked with arranging international tours for African American artists. It was in part as a result of this clandestine campaign that Leontyne Price, Dizzy Gillespie, Marian Anderson and William Warfield were first seen on the international stage. *Porgy and Bess*, described by one strategist as the 'Great Negro folk opera', was also given covert support and toured Western Europe, South America and then the Soviet bloc for more than a decade as a 'living demonstration of the American Negro as part of America's cultural life'.[14] In addition to arranging tours, the cultural cold warriors used Voice Of America (VOA) radio to spread their message further still. In the words of a New York Times article dated 6 November 1955:

America's secret weapon is a blue note in a minor key. Right now its most effective ambassador is Louis (Satchmo) Armstrong. A telling propaganda line is the hopped up tempo of a Dixieland band heard on the Voice Of America in far-off Tangier . . . American jazz has now become a universal language. It knows no national boundaries, but everybody knows where it comes from and where to look for more.[15]

Tellingly, the VOA's music consultant in the 1960s, Willis Conover, described the station as 'the radio arm of the United States Information Agency (USIA)', which, according to Frank Kofsky, supervised 'the dissemination of pro-US and anti-socialist propaganda throughout the world'.[16] Listeners hooked by the great music were reeled-in with news items promoting the American government's perspective on world events. Ghana's first president, Kwame Nkrumah, described the USIA broadcasts in Africa as 'the chief executor of U.S. psychological warfare [glorifying] the U.S. while attempting to discredit countries [like Ghana under Nkrumah] with an independent foreign policy'.[17]

*   *   *

The more I learned, the more a picture emerged that looks quite different from the one we're routinely presented with. Music, we are led to believe, is 'just' entertainment. It may be ubiquitous, much loved and very profitable for some in the business – but it won't change the world. To think it might is an infantile delusion. But secretly, rulers have always understood the power of music. They recognise that culture is a key battleground in the fight for hearts and minds – an important tool not only to make money, but also to manufacture consent.

CHAPTER THREE

Partying for Your Right to Fight

Let's look at the terrain on which the political contestation of culture takes place. The first point to make is obvious: money talks. The playing field is steeply sloped in favour of the owners of national radio stations, daily newspapers, record companies, digital platforms, management agencies, festivals, booking agencies and so on. If an artist is thought to be too politically controversial, the industry gatekeepers can refuse them entry, shelve their releases, and decline to book them. Sometimes this will take the form of official 'blacklists', but more commonly it'll be a subtle side-lining of a career. However, despite the long odds, a lot can be achieved with some determination and creativity. The relationship between economics and culture is complex – just because a shadowy economic elite formally own the culture industries, it doesn't mean they'll get it all their own way. After all, to appeal to a mass audience, music must speak to the lived experiences and feelings of that audience. People don't always want to hear a message drafted or approved by the ruling class. If they did, the soundtrack to our lives would probably be a sequence of Gary Barlow composed corporate jingles occasionally punctuated by 'God Save the Queen'. Instead we want to hear music that speaks of our trials, tribulations, hopes, fears, heartaches, loves, losses, highs and lows. To remain profitable, the mainstream music industry must give us at least something of what we want. In that 'something' lies opportunity.

We can also draw hope from the way that limited means often leads to important innovation – money gives you power, but those lacking it often have the best ideas. When people's desires to express themselves meet technological or economic constraints, creative solutions are found. An example close to my heart is the origin of the overdriven sound of the electric guitar. Early experiments in the sound began following budget cuts to the swing bands of the 1930s. Guitarists were initially trying to imitate the sound of the saxophone – a consequence of the real saxophonists being laid-off during the Great Depression. We see the same sort of creative innovation when people are faced with political repression. Perhaps the most remarkable example is the history of carnival. On a recent visit to the Caribbean island of Trinidad, I learned that carnival's many rich traditions arise directly from a clash between ordinary people determined to reclaim some time, space and pleasure in their lives, and a ruling class who fear them.

My education began at Port of Spain's 'Carnival Village', where I met Barry, an elderly and rather irascible representative of Trinidad and Tobago's steel pan union. On discovering my nationality, a glint appeared in his eye. It came, I soon learned, not from any fondness for the British, but rather from thoughts of a much celebrated riot against them. Barry extended a bony finger in the direction of an empty seat, which I took as an invitation to join him, and with a look somewhere between stoic pride and studied disinterest, told me the history of carnival. The tradition of pre-lent masquerade, he began, arrived on the island with French 'planters' forced from Haiti by the revolution of 1791–1804. Predictably, slaves were excluded from the festivities. Following the formal ending of slavery in the 1830s, the former slaves and other workers decided to make their own parallel celebration called 'Canboulay'. Barry speculated that the name came from the French for burnt cane: *cannes brulées*. People would set fire to the crop symbolising their oppression and parade into town in celebration. Masks were worn to disguise identities, thwarting the ruler's attempts to pick out individuals for retribution. When, in 1846, the authorities banned masks, mud and paint were used instead. Carnival-goers cover themselves in mud and paint to this day, during the *J'ouvert* (daybreak) procession.

The musical origins of carnival lay in West African 'kaiso' – narrative songs led by griots or 'chantwells', long used by slaves to mock their oppressors. Unsurprisingly, the plantocracy hated Canboulay, seeing it as a powerful symbolic challenge to their authority. A report commissioned in the 1840s concluded:

> We will not dwell on the disgusting and indecent scenes that were enacted in our streets – we will not say how many we saw in a state so nearly approaching nudity as to outrage decency and shock modesty . . . but we will say at once that the custom of keeping Carnival by allowing the lower order of society to run about the streets in wretched masquerade belongs to other days, and ought to be abolished in our own.[1]

Over the next decades, more and more restrictions were imposed on carnival until, in 1881, the British colonial rulers tried to stop it altogether. Captain Baker and his troops violently rounded on the crowd with truncheons, but people fought back leading to the legendary Canboulay riot. After several hours, the police were forced to retreat and carnival was saved. Ruling class opinion was divided about what to do next. An investigation by R.G. Hamilton for the colonial office in London advised:

> However objectionable some of the features of carnival are, I believe it is looked forward to as the only holiday of the year by a large number of the working population of the town, who derive amusements from it and I think to stop it altogether would be a measure that would

justly be regarded as harsh and might lead to serious dissatisfaction on the part of the working classes.[2]

In 1883 rulers finally agreed a new strategy – they would ban not the procession, but its musical heartbeat, the djembe-style 'skin drum'. Musicians responded creatively, reasoning that if drums were prohibited they would simply find an alternative. They set about exploring the percussive qualities of bamboo – an abundant natural resource on the island. It seemed that different lengths and thicknesses produced different tones when banged on the ground and hit with a piece of hard wood. Bamboo groups, or 'tamboo bamboo' (from *tambour* – French for drum) soon became the sound of carnival across the island. Players tended to come from the rougher parts of town and running street battles between rival groups were commonplace. But it's unlikely that public safety was uppermost in the minds of the authorities when, in 1934, they stepped in again, this time to ban the tamboo bamboo.

Trinidadian calls for self-rule and universal suffrage had been growing throughout the first decades of the twentieth century. Troops were sent to break a strike by dockers in 1919, and with the hardships of the Great Depression spreading to the islands during the 1930s, militant nationalists' ideas were gaining ground. The colonial regime became nervous and sought to keep people off the streets, fearful as to how things might escalate in the increasingly politicised atmosphere. In 1936 they introduced Ordinance 23, banning suggestive dancing, profane songs, or songs 'that insult members of the upper class'.[3] The outbreak of the Second World War gave them a pretext to stop carnival altogether. Musicians bided their time, exploring possible alternatives to bamboo. When the US joined the war, its navy commandeered large parts of Trinidad, littering the island with huge numbers of oil drums. In slum areas such as Laventille in East Port of Spain, musicians got to work, the more attentive of whom noticed that the tone produced at the start of a playing session changed as the drum became dented. Over time, a tuning system developed and something similar to the now familiar tuned steel pan was revealed to amazed revellers at Trinidad's VE Day celebrations in 1945.

The much loved steel pan – one of the few acoustic instruments to have been invented in the twentieth century – exists only because of the creativity and determination of ordinary people facing political repression. The instrument symbolises our indefatigable desire to express ourselves through music.

Barry went on to describe how in 1951 an all-star delegation of pan players was sent to represent Trinidad and Tobago at the Festival of Britain, starting a love affair with the instrument in 'the mother country'. Britons swooned at the sound of the steel pan orchestra. Radio broadcasts and a three-week tour were hastily arranged. Significantly, one member of the orchestra, Sterling Betancourt, decided to make London his home. Betancourt taught pan to jazz musician Russell Henderson, who promptly formed the Russell Henderson Steel Band. On August bank holiday 1964, a year after Trinidad and Tobago gained independence, the band performed at a street party in West London. It had been organised by Rhuane Laslett, a social worker and community activist. She wanted to provide a fun day out for local children whose parents couldn't afford to take them on holiday. Lloyd Bradley described the modest affair:

> Far from being any sort of Caribbean celebration, it was simply about the area itself . . . the children who attended were a junior United Nations of English, Polish, Irish, African, Russian, Portuguese and West Indian. The entertainment laid on for them was equally varied, including a donkey cart donated by market traders from Portobello Market, an African drummer with an elephant's foot drum . . . a clown, a box of false moustaches and the Russell Henderson Steel Band.[4]

At some point, the pan men decided to lead an impromptu procession through the surrounding streets. As Russell Henderson recalled:

> It was real exciting and people were swept up with it, so we just kept on going... It was like we were Pied

Pipers; the police did nothing because they thought if they stopped us there might be trouble. A lot of English people joined it too, most of them were happy to see it, but some didn't know what it was – they saw so many West Indians on a parade like this and they thought it was a demonstration. They were shouting at us 'What have you got to demonstrate about? If you want to complain go back to your own country!' The thing was in those days we did go on demonstrations, we used to go on Ban the Bomb marches, and when they come up from Aldermaston we used to join in at Kensington and go up to Hyde Park with them. So some people thought this was the steel band doing a demonstration again.[5]

From those spontaneous steps would grow the annual Notting Hill Carnival – now the largest street festival in the northern hemisphere attracting over a million revellers every year. Steel pan orchestras remain central to the celebrations. How many of the party people know, I wonder, that the event owes its very existence to a more or less unbroken sequence of acts of political defiance and ingenuity stretching back to the Haitian revolution of 1791?

* * *

Usually music and politics are presented as two different spheres. Different subjects at school, different parts of the newspaper, separate, discrete. Of course, some artists are known for being political. And some political gatherings will include a bit of rousing music to introduce a speaker, or a gig – usually at the end of the day for participants to relax at with a drink. But on the whole we're led to believe that politics takes place in parliament and occasionally on picket lines and demonstrations, while culture is synonymous with recreation and entertainment. However, the story of carnival underlines the fact that culture and politics are intimately linked. Whether we realise it or not, many of the pleasures and parties we take for granted are the result of political struggles. And it's only a small exaggeration to say that political struggles are sometimes fought on impromptu dance-floors, and won or lost according to who has the best tunes.

CHAPTER FOUR

Getting Political

Highlife to Soul

A few years ago, I was lucky enough to be asked to travel to Paris to work on an album by a Senegalese kora player called Doudou Cissoko. The kora is a beautiful 21-string instrument often described as the West African harp. I'd been in love with its sound ever since I first heard it on the headphones of a listening post in the 'world music' section of a record shop when I was young. Doudou and I quickly became good friends. During those Paris sessions he told me about a generation of political leaders who openly embraced the power of music.

Prior to colonialism and the transatlantic slave trade, music formed part of the fabric of traditional class society in West Africa. Musicians, known as *griots* or *jalis*, relied on patronage from wealthy individuals. It's not surprising therefore, that many of their songs were written to flatter their paymasters. However, communities also expected musicians to bring any concerns to their bosses' attention – to be 'truth tellers'. This was music as a form of mediation. Singers reinforced the power and status of the rich, but also reminded them of their obligations to the rest of society. Music contributed to a dialogue aiming for social peace – its role was conservative.

Colonialism completely undermined societies across West Africa. Traditional rulers found themselves taking orders from a new group of outsiders. That shift in political power changed the role played by music. What once contributed to social harmony started to represent nationalist, or indeed pan-African cultural pride, and the movement for self-determination. For the most part the movement was led not by musicians, but organised workers. Industrial action had been fomenting across the region since the early 1900s. In 1945, the first general strike in Nigerian history paralysed the colonial machine for six weeks, and in 1947, a railway strike in Senegal became a major factor in the birth of the nationalist movement. But politics has always been closely linked with the arts in West Africa. When Senegal gained independence in 1960, it was a poet, Léopold Senghor, who was elected president. Senghor chose the kora as a new symbol of national pride and one of the country's best known kora players, Soundinoulou Cissoko – my friend Doudou's father – became a cultural ambassador.

Although organised workers led the liberation movements, musicians did more than just celebrate independence after it had been achieved. Many also played a direct role in the struggle – particularly those playing popular music in the urban centres. Ghanaian highlife, a guitar-led dance music that became influential across the region, was initially associated with palm wine and parties. By the late 1940s, it started to reflect the growing support for Ghana's movement for self-determination led by the charismatic Kwame Nkrumah. Groups started to rename themselves – the 'Burma Jokers' became the 'Ghana Trio' following the pivotal 1948 Accra riots, provoked by the killing of four peaceful protestors by colonial police. The African Brothers took their name following then-President Nkrumah's initiation of the Organisation of African Unity in 1963. Musicians elsewhere sent messages of solidarity. Trinidadian calypsonian Young Tiger exported 20,000 copies of the song 'Freedom for Ghana' to West Africa and the king of calypso, Lord Kitchener, enjoyed huge success with 'Birth of Ghana', celebrating the nation's independence in 1957. Nkrumah welcomed this support and his Convention People's Party promoted a number of tours and concerts before and after independence. Nkrumah saw culture as a crucial cornerstone of the new independent nation and encouraged artists, choreographers, writers and intellectuals of the West African diaspora to settle in Ghana.

So far so good – except not all West Africans felt empowered by the changes. Many of the political parties fighting for independence described themselves as practising some sort of 'Marxism-Leninism'. But in practise they didn't really want to see a transfer of power to the people – they wanted an African elite to take over on behalf of the people. Increasingly the new governments sought to rein in militant workers' movements and reassure foreign investors. As a result, though ordinary West Africans were delighted to see the end of colonial rule, many felt the new regimes didn't really represent them. Too little had actually changed. Young West Africans, in particular, were frustrated with how many of their parents' generation appeared to simply copy the ways of the colonialists – they were trying to be 'more English than the English' or 'more French than the French'. What's more, they didn't have much interest in the traditional music officially promoted in countries like Senegal. Even the highlife favoured by Nkrumah seemed outdated. Instead they looked for new music and styles to reflect their more radical attempts to forge a new identity in the postcolonial world. They certainly didn't want to look to the youth cultures of the old colonial countries for inspiration. Instead, in the late 1960s, a new cultural movement emerged that looked across the Atlantic to the black diaspora – in particular to the Caribbean and the USA.

For many young West Africans, this was *consciously* political and progressive. They saw reggae, and most importantly American soul, as music of resistance to racism, colonialism and the conservative values of their parents. The highlife band Jaguar Jokers, and many like them, started to dress in sequinned jump-suits and cover

James Brown's 'Say It Loud – I'm Black and I'm Proud'.
Bands that didn't adopt American styles started to lose
audiences to the new soul covers bands or 'copyright
bands' as they were known. Malick Sidibé's wonderful
photos from the 1970s show how popular American
styles were in Mali. Malian filmmaker Manthia Diawara
described the scene:

> For me and many of my friends, to be liberated was to
> be exposed to more R&B songs and to be au courant of
> the latest exploits of Muhammad Ali, George Jackson,
> Angela Davis, Malcolm X and Martin Luther King
> Jr. These were becoming an alternate cultural capital
> for the African youth . . . enabling us to subvert the
> hegemony of Francité after independence.[1]

This was precisely the time many African Americans
were, at least symbolically, looking to Africa. They'd
heard Marcus Garvey, W.E.B. Du Bois and Malcolm
X and wanted to embrace an African identity in order
to distance themselves from the values of racist white
America. So when Africans looked longingly to America
for freedom, they found African Americans looking
longingly back. African Americans started to visit West
Africa in delegations organised by groups such as CORE
(Congress of Racial Equality), leading jokers in Accra to
ask: 'How do you tell the African Americans apart from
their Ghanaian hosts? . . . the African Americans are the

ones wearing their Ghanaian hosts' traditional cloth and flowing *Agbadas* and the Ghanaians are the ones in the sharp American suits!'[2]

However, not all West Africans swooned at the sound of soul. One Nigerian journalist felt compelled to ask:

How on earth a Nigerian could condescend to 'soul'. As the Nigerian James Browns wish us to believe, this soul thing is more than a dance. It is a fraternity, it is black smoothness, negroid rhythm ... the lot. I ask you – what is negroid about soul? The Black Africans in Brazil use African musical instruments and really sweat it out to Yemoja, the long-forgotten Yoruba goddess ... What the American Negroes are doing, and converting young Nigerians to, is a perversion of the African beat.[3]

Some started to question the scene's political impact. Colonial European ways had been swept aside, but in their place was another import – one that sometimes seemed to prioritise sequin bellbottoms and good times over people power. Were Africa's soul sisters and brothers keener on getting down and boogying than standing up and fighting? Political leaders became concerned that cultural trends reflected a creeping new imperialism. What starts with James Brown's 'Sex Machine' might end with Richard Nixon's B52s – or at least the rule of US capital. It was on this basis that Tanzania's premier Julius Nyerere banned soul music in 1969. We'll never know whether

Ghana's President Nkrumah had similar plans. In 1965, he had almost single-handedly engineered the expulsion of apartheid South Africa from the Commonwealth and in the same year called for pan-African unity to destroy neo-colonialism, in his much publicised book *Neo Colonialism: The Last Stage of Imperialism*. The US reacted by withdrawing $35 million of aid from Ghana and doubling the CIA presence in Accra overnight. A military coup followed in 1966 while Nkrumah was on a state visit to China. He never returned to Ghana. In 1971, the country celebrated its independence day with a huge soul concert in Black Star Square, featuring Wilson Pickett, Ike and Tina Turner, Roberta Flack, the Staple Singers and Santana.

However well-intentioned, Nyerere's banning of soul music should make us nervous – government bans on music are rarely a good thing. Besides, even if we accept the logic, such top-down attempts to control culture in the national interest seldom seem to be sustainable – remember those futile attempts to ban Beatlemania (Back) in the USSR? A much better solution to the political ambiguity of the new scene was offered by Nigerian musician Fela Kuti. Fela mixed the best aspects of soul and funk with highlife and other West African sounds. With the addition of overtly political lyrics, a new genre called Afrobeat was born. It's worth saying a few words about Fela's story and music, since they clearly capture the complexities and contradictions of postcolonial West Africa.

In his ground-breaking book *The Wretched of the Earth*, Frantz Fanon describes three phases that many of the most important anti-colonial leaders, or 'native intellectuals', pass through:

1. Strong identification with the colonial master usually following a period of education in the colonial centre.
2. A reaction to the first phase during which the intellectual uncritically celebrates his native society rejecting anything associated with the colonial master.
3. The native intellectual outgrows the romanticisation of the previous phase, sharpen their critical thinking and direct it towards his or her native society.

All three phases can be found in Fela's life. Born in 1938 to a middle-class, left-leaning family, he pursued his dreams of becoming a musician with a period of study in London. While officially attending the Trinity College of Music, he reportedly spent most of his time playing jazz in clubs such as Ronnie Scott's. He returned to Nigeria in 1963 to work with his latin and calypso-inflected highlife band Koola Lobitos. At this time, he showed little interest in politics. But in 1969, during an otherwise fairly disastrous tour of the US, he started a relationship with a woman called Sandra Smith. Smith was a Black Panther and had spent time in prison after an alleged assault on a police officer during the 1967 LA riots. In one of many ironies in his story, it was Smith who introduced Fela to the writings of Nkrumah, Malcolm X, Angela Davis and others. Some writers say that Fela needed to go to the US to discover Africa. Certainly the trip was a key politicising experience. He returned to Nigeria radicalised. He changed the name of his band first to Nigeria 70 and later to Africa 70 as his commitment to pan-Africanism grew. Songs from this period such as 'Buy Africa' and 'Black Man's Cry' articulated his new-found African pride.

Fela dismissed praise singers as beggars and instead tapped into a lesser-known tradition that he labelled 'abuse singing'. He charged the old colonial powers and their multinational companies with keeping Africans impoverished. But increasingly he saw the military government of Nigeria as complicit. The authorities responded by attacking and imprisoning him several times.

He resolved the dilemma of language, faced by most postcolonial writers, by neither adopting local languages that might limit his audience (in his case Yoruba) nor by using the language of the coloniser (in Nigeria's case English). Instead he opted for 'pidgin' and slang familiar to a mass audience. Fela was consciously reaching out to the poor and working class. As a result, his fame soared during the late 1970s and he declared several times he would run for president.

His uncompromising attacks on corruption and hypocrisy weren't just a challenge for the Nigerian authorities. They also forced black nationalists to look beyond an analysis of oppression based solely on race. After all, Fela highlighted that although white rule had ended in Nigeria, poverty and violent repression hadn't. In an interview for the 1980 documentary film *Music is the Weapon*, he argued:

In Nigeria they come and do apartheid committee . . . They're meeting about Namibia in Nigeria . . . How can Nigeria be talking about South Africa? South Africa is *better* than Nigeria. I know so! Look . . . We are saying whites are mistreating blacks in South Africa. OK. That is bad. That is racism . . . they have a reason to do it. Blacks are mistreating blacks in Nigeria . . . What is the reason!? That's worse. Police beat people on the streets like dogs. I mean in South Africa they do it, but they know they face public criticisms, so they watch themselves to do it. But in Nigeria . . . America talks about Nigeria like it is the greatest African country, but Nigeria is the *worst* African country. The *worst* things are happening – *worse* than South Africa.[4]

Fela was a bohemian, maverick and punk provocateur. He forged his own idiosyncratic, often contradictory political path. He failed to see a problem with the sexist depiction of women at his club, the Shrine, and in some of his songs. This was particularly surprising given that he always remained close to his mother, Funmilayo Kuti, who was a leading Nigerian socialist and fighter for women's liberation. It's also said that Fela treated his musicians badly and ruled the commune in which he lived with an iron fist. But for all his shortcomings, he did successfully open up a space in West African popular music for an all-out assault on colonialism, neo-colonialism and corruption. Perhaps most importantly, he demonstrated that uncompromising political lyrics could sit on the irresistible grooves of dance-floor fillers.

Parties Behind Parties

Leaders of all political persuasions recognise the power of culture. The more I learned, the more I found that this has always been the case. From pharaohs to feudal lords, muftis to maharajahs, republicans to royals, rulers always have a music policy. All have given patronage to some musicians and many have tried to suppress the music of others.

But what of the musicians? How have they made their opinions known? We've already seen John Lennon subvert a state broadcast; musicians in West Africa join struggles for independence and Trinidadian singers send messages of solidarity. We've seen American stars inspire a generation to be Black and Proud and Fela Kuti assert his right to challenge corruption and state violence whatever the ethnicity of its perpetrators. What other examples can we find of artists acting in a consciously political way? What inspired them to do so and what impact did their music have?

Since 'Free Nelson Mandela' had set me on my journey into the world of music and politics, I decided to ask its writer, Jerry Dammers, about the story behind the seminal song. It began in the summer of 1983, when he attended a concert at Alexander Palace organised by an exiled South African musician called Julian Bahula. The gig was a celebration of the 65th birthday of jailed African National Congress (ANC) leader Nelson Mandela, whom Dammers had never heard of. The night made a big impression and he left determined to learn more and to act. The result was the Special AKA's 'Free Nelson Mandela', released in March 1984. Soon after its release, Dammers was called by Danny Tambo – the son of the exiled president of the ANC, Oliver Tambo. He persuaded Dammers to help organise Artists Against Apartheid UK. Over the next few years, the organisation successfully staged numerous concerts across the country to raise awareness about South African apartheid, including one on Clapham Common attended by some 200,000 people. The popularity of that event encouraged its organisers to think even bigger, leading to Nelson Mandela's 70th birthday concert, organised by the Anti-Apartheid Movement (AAM) and held at Wembley Stadium in 1988. The concert featured some of the biggest artists of the time including Stevie Wonder, Whitney Houston, Tracy Chapman, Miriam Makeba, George Michael, Dire Straits and Youssou N'Dour. Dammers took to the stage to lead an electrifying performance of 'Free Nelson Mandela'. The event was screened by nearly 100 national broadcasters to an estimated 600 million people around the world. The ever modest Dammers concluded by reminding me of the little known South African musician who started it all: 'which proves that big things can grow from any action – such as Julian Bahula's initiative.'

What struck me about the story was the active cooperation between artists and political organisations – in this case the ANC, Artists Against Apartheid and the Anti-Apartheid Movement. Political organisations need good tunes. But good tunes also need political organisations. Without the ANC's suggestion of a broader campaign, the impact of Dammers' song might have dissipated, rather than being channelled into a movement that eventually grabbed the attention of millions and arguably helped change the world.

The importance of political organisation is also underlined by the tale of one of the most powerful songs of the twentieth century. 'Strange Fruit' is the haunting meditation on lynching made famous by Billie Holiday. The great jazz drummer Max Roach described the impact of the song on its release in 1939:

When she recorded it, it was more than revolutionary. She made a statement that we all felt as black folks. No one was speaking out. She became one of the fighters, this beautiful lady who could sing and make you feel things. She became a voice of black people and they loved this woman.[5]

White audiences understood its significance too. As Samuel Grafton wrote in the New York Post:

It is as if a game of let's pretend had ended and a blues singer who had been hiding her true sorrow in a set of love ditties had lifted the curtain and told us what it was that made her cry ... The polite conversations between race and race are gone ... If the anger of the exploited ever mounts high enough in the South, it now has its Marseillaise.[6]

The song was written by a Jewish schoolteacher and Communist Party member called Abel Meeropol. His motives for doing so were clear: 'I wrote "Strange Fruit" because I hated lynching and I hate injustice and I hate the people who perpetuate it.'[7] Holiday's version of the song would never have existed without the help of political activists and organisations of the left. Before she heard the song, it had been performed by a number of progressive singers including an African American quartet at a fundraiser for the anti-fascists during the

Spanish Civil War. The co-producer of that event was a left-wing activist called Robert Gordon who also booked acts for the radical nightspot Café Society in Greenwich Village. Café Society's star attraction in December 1938 was Billie Holiday who had recently left Artie Shaw's band. Shaw, the first white bandleader to hire a black singer full-time, was criticised by music industry executives who wanted a more 'mainstream' singer. Audiences in the South were also hostile to Holiday and she finally quit the band following the humiliating experience of having to take the freight elevator to a gig at the Abraham Lincoln hotel in New York, due to a ban on black people using the front door and guest elevator. Café Society was one of the few racially integrated hangouts in New York City. Gordon suggested that Meeropol should stop by the club and it was there that he sat at the piano and played 'Strange Fruit' to Holiday for the first time. Her performances of the song were soon the talk of the city. The English jazz writer Leonard Feather visited Café Society in April 1939. Writing in *Melody Maker*, he described how Holiday 'stood in a small jet of light, turned on her most wistful expression . . . and sang a number especially written for her, "Strange Fruit", a grim and moving piece about lynching down South.' He also noted, 'With young left-wingers behind the scenes, it is no wonder that the music is swell here, and that the usual ruling against the acceptance of coloured people as customers does not prevail.'[8]

Columbia Records, Holiday's label in the late 1930s, were nervous about what they saw as the radical politics of the song and wanted nothing to do with it. It was left to Commodore Records – a small left-wing label dedicated to promoting progressive artists – to record and release it.

Absolute Oblivion

It seems that political organisations – sometimes openly, sometimes secretly – take culture very seriously. Progressive political organisations have helped to promote artists and songs that the mainstream music industry wouldn't (initially) go near. In so doing they've helped to enrich culture and change society.

However, it's important to remember that musicians are just as capable of being on the wrong side of history. Either out of greed, fear, or conviction, musicians have always been found to provide the most backward elements of society with tunes to rally their troops. Some of the most disturbing examples took place during the dictatorships of twentieth-century Europe. As author and *New Yorker* music critic Alex Ross points out:

For anyone who cherishes the notion that there is some inherent spiritual goodness in artists of great talent, the era of Stalin and Hitler is disillusioning. Not only did composers fail to rise up en masse against totalitarianism, but many actively welcomed it. In the capitalist free-for-all of the twenties, they had contended with technologically enhanced mass culture, which introduced a new aristocracy of movie stars, pop musicians, and celebrities without portfolio. Having long depended on the largesse of the Church, the upper classes, and the high bourgeoisie, composers suddenly found themselves, in the Jazz Age, without obvious means of support. Some fell to dreaming of a political knight in shining armour who would come to their aid. The dictators played that role to perfection.[9]

Stalin and Hitler took a keen interest in music. Both bestowed privileges on composers who could create the right tone for their propaganda – and both were quick to terminate the careers of those who did not. Few composers were likely to have seen them as 'knights in shining armour' for long. One badly-received opera could land you in a gulag, prison camp or worse. Shostakovich knew this well. In 1936, more than a decade before the humiliating trip to New York City described earlier, Stalin and the Politburo turned up to see his production of Lady Macbeth. When the composer took his bow after the third act, eyewitnesses described him as being 'white as a sheet'. He was right to be afraid. Stalin found the production vulgar and the state newspaper *Pravda* reviewed the piece under the headline 'Muddle instead of Music'. It condemned the music as 'deliberately dissonant' and concluded with the chilling assessment that the composer was playing a game 'that may end very badly'. In a decision that probably saved his life, Shostakovich withdrew his Fourth Symphony, which was already in production. In 1937, he regained official favour and public acclaim with a more musically conservative Fifth Symphony. But not everyone thinks he had been completely cowed. Listen to the finale of the Fifth Symphony. Arguably, it is by his standards, bland, formulaic and pedestrian. Was he simply playing it safe or is there sarcasm in the all too predictable bombast and pomp? Do we hear in those final bars the musical equivalent of a backside bared at the Politburo?

When later asked why Shostakovich had been targeted in the 'Muddle Instead of Music' piece, the editor of *Pravda* gave a fascinating reply: 'We had to begin with somebody. Shostakovich was the most famous, and a blow against him would create immediate repercussions and would make his imitators in music and elsewhere sit up and take notice.'[10]

It's not only totalitarian regimes where the powerful make examples of certain artists in order to create a climate of fear in which others will play it safe and self-censor. Certainly the stakes were higher under Stalin's Terror, but even in liberal democracies today artists often refrain from making political statements because they are worried their careers may be derailed. The Texas based Dixie Chicks were on tour in Europe in early 2003, as opposition to the Iraq war was building.

They saw the protests culminate in millions taking to the streets around the world on 15 February. In London, two million marched making the day the biggest political protest in British history. Less than a month later, nine days before the war began, the band played at London's Shepherds Bush Empire. They took the opportunity to express their solidarity with the protests and added that they were ashamed of their President. The crowd cheered, but when the statement was reported in the US the band were denounced on TV channels and radio stations across the country. Their cover of Fleetwood Mac's 'Landslide' dropped sharply in the Billboard Hot 100 chart, tickets sales slumped and concerts were cancelled. Shocked by the reaction, the band issued an apology, but the commercial damage was already done. Bruce Springsteen and Madonna were among a number of artists who defended the Texans' right to express themselves freely. But tellingly, on witnessing the backlash, Madonna postponed the release of her album *American Life* in order to shoot a new video. The original cut between scenes of war, catwalk models in military garb and seemingly traumatised dancer/soldiers hiding in toilet cubicles. It ended with Madonna throwing a hand grenade at a President Bush lookalike. The replacement video simply had Madonna singing to camera in front of various national flags. Such examples abound. Fear leads artists to create work that abstains from social comment, papers over contradictions, and fails to engage honestly with feelings. Rulers demonise dissenters in order to win battles before they are fought.

Hitler also understood the power of culture. As the Russian revolutionary Leon Trotsky's illuminating commentaries on the rise of the Nazis described, the Führer's success depended not just on paralysis in the political mainstream and the tactical disasters of German communism, but also on cultural and emotional manipulation – 'soul-massage' as Goebbels put it. Musicians were complicit. The ground-breaking composer Richard Strauss was one of a number directly recruited by the Third Reich. Others apparently provided inspiration. On more than one occasion Hitler claimed that Wagner's *Rienzi* had inspired him to take up politics. There was also more than a passing resemblance between the Führer's idiosyncratic hand gestures and the conducting style of (Jewish composer) Gustav Mahler, whom he had seen conduct Wagner's *Tristan und Isolde* in Vienna in 1906. As Ross points out:

> There is a strange displacement going on here, given that a Jew occupied the podium during what may have been the most tremendous musical experience of Hitler's life. Was Mahler a tormenting symbol of Jewish power amid Hitler's failures? Or did the young man identify with Mahler's aura, his ability to command forces with a wave of his arms?[11]

The Nazi's legacy was one of devastation for the music of Europe as well as its people. As well as murdering millions, the Holocaust effectively wiped out entire schools of composition that had thrived between the wars in cities such as Berlin, Vienna and Prague.

Some European composers did make principled stands against the enveloping darkness. In the backrooms of coffee shops in occupied Warsaw, Andrzej Panufnik and Witold Lutolawski brazenly led songs of resistance and performed banned works by Mendelssohn, Gershwin and Chopin. In Athens, the composer Iannis Xenakis took up arms against the occupation. His story is revealing. It underlines the uncomfortable truth that it wasn't only Europe's dictators who had contempt for the will of ordinary people.

Xenakis is considered by many to be one of the most important postwar avant-garde composers. Born in Romania in 1922, he travelled to Greece as a ten-year-old to attend a boarding school on the Aegean island of Spetsai. In 1938, on the eve of the Second World War, he moved to Athens to go to university, but his studies were cut short when the armies of Nazi Germany and fascist Italy rolled into town. It was the start of an occupation that would last more than three years. Xenakis joined the National Liberation Front (EAM) who organised demonstrations, strikes, sabotage actions and armed resistance against the occupiers. By 1943, the EAM claimed a membership of two million, nearly a third of the population, with activists and supporters organised in popular committees in every town and village. In the autumn of 1944, Xenakis and his comrades succeeded in driving out the Axis forces. You may think that British Prime Minister Winston Churchill would have sent a message of congratulations. Instead he deployed British troops to crush the victorious left and restore the monarchy. A state of emergency was imposed and Greece was plunged into civil war. The British teamed up with local fascists and Xenakis found himself under attack once again. As he sheltered in a house with a comrade, a British tank shell landed on the building killing his friend and blowing half of Xenakis' face off. It's a miracle he survived, but the nightmare was far from over. As soon as the British and their Greek clients had gained control of the country a 'White Terror' was unleashed. Between February and July 1945, mass arrests were made of some 20,000 EAM members and sympathisers, and following a succession of show trials, nearly 3,000 were sentenced to death. Fearing for his life, Xenakis went into hiding. In November 1947, he fled Greece through Italy to Paris. In a late interview, Xenakis described his guilt at leaving the country. Those feelings underpinned his devotion to composition:

> For years I was tormented by guilt at having left the country for which I'd fought. I left my friends – some were in prison, others were dead, some managed to

escape. I felt I was in debt to them and that I had to repay that debt. And I felt I had a mission. I had to do something important to regain the right to live. It wasn't just a question of music – it was something much more significant.[12]

Xenakis never set out to be a political artist. Nor did he ever claim to be making political statements with his work. But listen to the first major piece he wrote after the war – *Metastaseis* – and decide for yourself whether it could have been conceived by someone who hadn't witnessed humanity's capacity for amorality, violence and destruction.

Xenakis wasn't the only composer to have experienced first-hand the horrors of war. Karlheinz Stockhausen worked as a stretcher-bearer for a mobile hospital behind the Western front. He later recalled his attempts to revive soldiers who had fallen victim to Allied bombs: 'I would try to find an opening in the mouth for a straw in order to pour some liquid into these men, whose bodies were still moving, but there was only a yellow ball-like mass where the face should have been.'[13]

Bernd Alois Zimmermann and Luciano Berio both fought as young conscripts and the English composer Benjamin Britten was horrified by what he saw on a tour of defeated Germany with Yehudi Menuhin in July 1945. All were appalled that music had played a part in the carnage – marching men off to war and bolstering the claims of their leaders. A generation of composers felt it was their duty to ensure this could never happen again. The Western canon that had yielded so easily to the demands of demagogues needed to be torn up. New music, they determined, must reject all notions of heroism, righteousness, conquest or pride. Traditional musical structures and harmony were eschewed and increasingly composers abstained from trying to convey universal human truths – fearful perhaps of what those truths might be. Many even retreated from their own subjectivity, towards ever more rigidly adhered to serialism and randomly generated 'chance' compositions. Adorno summed up the situation in his *Philosophy of New Music*: '[New music] has taken upon itself all the darkness and guilt of the world. All its happiness comes in the perception of misery, all its beauty comes in the rejection of beauty's illusion . . . New music spontaneously takes aim at the final condition of absolute oblivion. It is the true message in a bottle.'[14]

CHAPTER FIVE

Unity Lost

We've seen how determined people can be to express themselves through music, even in very difficult circumstances. Rulers have tried to control it and radicals to reclaim it from the rulers. The political power of music became so evident to a generation of European composers that they got spooked; afraid of the forces they might unwittingly unleash. The result was a postwar avant-garde which was manipulated and meddled with by agents of Cold War antagonists. Meanwhile mass audiences moved towards pop, which was also politically contested in all the ways we've seen. It seems that whatever musical style we choose, they all emerge from and are subject to ongoing struggles. The complex, often hidden, political tug-of-war persists. Culture is a battleground. But even though the battle continues regardless of our musical preferences, those preferences are still revealing. In a hotel room somewhere in Norway, I was reminded that different musical sounds and songs offer valuable insights into the societies in which they're heard.

Unable to sleep, I'd reached for the remote to try to get the overcomplicated 'entertainment system' to show signs of life. After scrolling through seemingly endless onscreen menus, I eventually found an episode of *Human Planet*. The fascinating show featured a people known as the Bayaka who survive to this day as traditional foragers in the dense tropical rainforests of Africa's Congo Basin. The narrator said that the Bayaka consider *music* to be the greatest gift from the forest. From the shared task of washing clothes in a river evolved an ability to rhythmically slap and cup the surface of the water, making the river itself into a percussion instrument, and from imitating the sounds of the animals in the forest comes a unique and beautiful style of communal singing. The Bayaka are an example of a tribe continuing a way of life that preceded class society. There was a time when all humans lived as they do – foraging together, sharing food and shelter and working communally without class divisions or private property. They remind us that it is in the intimate connection between human beings and nature that music has its origins.

As a wall of synthesised noise hit me from the monitors at soundcheck the next day, I reflected on how far culture has travelled since those days when the sounds of the natural world made up our music. One of the first staging posts in that long journey was the development of agriculture. Its tools became the instruments of music. Take the Hamitic peoples of the Nile Valley who have been agricultural-ists since antiquity. They tied together two sticks which were rhythmically clapped to chase pests away from their crops. At the end of the working day, the same clapping tool accompanied ritual dances to ensure the fertility of the crops. The instrument is used to this day.[1]

Music was also closely linked to the task of putting food on the table in ancient China. On the change of seasons and often at forks in rivers, male and female choirs would gather to sing eight-syllable phrases back and forth in a kind of competition symbolising the two polar principles of the universe – yin and yang. It was thought that such rituals would encourage abundant crop yields. To ensure that a spiritual balance and harmony with nature was achieved, the singing was followed by sexual rites.

In the Javanese terraced paddy-fields of Southeast Asia, a new musical sound evolved with improvements in rice production. Hollow bamboo tubes were carefully arranged on pivots to draw water from irrigation channels, which when full, would tip forward supplying the field below. Once emptied, the carefully weighted tube would pivot back to its original position hitting a stone, thereby emitting a resonant knock at regular intervals. The purpose was to alert those tending the fields of any interruption to the flow of water, but the melodious sound inspired some farmers to experiment with different sized tubes and tilt intervals. The result was charmingly described by Peter Crossley-Holland:

> Here already we have a pointer to the modern south-east Asian orchestras of chimes and the fundamental

texture of their music: sounds and rhythms so varied and combined as to weave an intricate pattern and in so doing to lose their separate identities like threads in a cloth. And if, falling under the spell of such sounds continuously heard throughout long days in the fields, man lends his voice to the ensemble in a freely improvised melody – and for anyone with musical susceptibilities it is difficult to resist – a free creative element is added and the composition is complete.[2]

The American writer Sydney Finkelstein thought that art describes our collective experience of whichever stage of social development we find ourselves in:

There are many ways of recording the outer objective world which are not art: natural science, the writing of history, journalism, sociology, statistics, economics, photography used simply for documentary purposes. The unique quality of art, a quality which sometimes touched the above activities and makes them enter – accidentally, so to speak – the realm of art, is that it discloses the inner world, corresponding to the outer. In other words, it shows what it means to live at a certain moment, or stage of development, of social life and conquest of nature. It replaces fact with typicality. It discloses not an actual event but a pattern of outer movement, as a force operating on human hopes and feelings.[3]

So if music once spoke of our intimate connection with nature and the shared tasks of working the land, what does it tell us now?

Well, let's begin by looking at some songs we've all grown up with – songs that have helped to define popular culture over the past few decades – at least in the Western world. Table 1 shows the top ten highest earning songs of all time:[4]

Table 1   The top ten highest earning songs of all time

Song Title	Composer(s)	Publishing revenue
1. Happy Birthday	(credited to) the Hill Sisters	£30 million
2. White Christmas	Irving Berlin	£24 million
3. You've Lost That Lovin' Feelin	Barry Mann, Cynthia Weil and Phil Spector	£20.5 million
4. Yesterday	Paul McCartney (credited: Lennon and McCartney)	£19.5 million
5. Unchained Melody	Alex North and Hy Zaret	£18 million
6. Stand by Me	Ben E. King, Jerry Leiber and Mike Stoller	£17.5 million
7. Santa Claus is Coming to Town	Haven Gillespie and Fred J Coots	£16.5 million
8. Every Breath You Take	Sting	£13.5 million
9. Oh, Pretty Woman	Roy Orbison and Bill Dees	£13 million
10. The Christmas Song	Mel Tormé	£12.5 million

Certainly we see the enduring appeal of Christmas. The other songs, except for the anomalous number one, share themes of regret, loss and a yearning for things to be different. Even the top-selling Christmas song – Irving Berlin's 'White Christmas' – is steeped in melancholy and longing for times past. For Berlin the heartache was personal: his first-born child died a cot death on Christmas Day, over a decade before he wrote the hit. But the feeling resonated with millions of people who shared a nostalgic sense that something essential is missing in the modern world.

Many other hits also suggest that audiences identify with feelings of loneliness and a general sense of dissatisfaction or unease. It's certainly true of most of the artists I've worked with. The protagonist of Faithless' biggest hit describes himself as lonely, and desperately seeks release from 'Insomnia': 'Creaky noises make my skin creep, I need to get some sleep, I can't get no sleep.' Sinead O'Connor's bestseller is the Prince-penned lament to an absent lover, 'Nothing Compares 2 U'. In the video she sings directly to the camera as tears roll down her cheeks.

Recently, I've had the pleasure of working with another artist who enjoyed huge success in the late 1980s, Roland Gift of the Fine Young Cannibals. One line his fans always sing along with and are clearly moved by is the pathos-laden question from the hit 'Johnny Come Home': 'What is wrong in my life, that I must get drunk every night?' Even Dido's 'Thank You' is a celebration of a single remarkable day in an otherwise unfulfilling, dreary life. And it was the song's sombre sounding verse rather than the breezy chorus that was sampled by Eminem for 'Stan' – the macabre tale that introduced Dido to a mass audience.

I conducted a quick survey of the Billboard Hot 100 highest selling hits from the 1980s, 1990s and 2000s, placing each in a broad category according to their main lyrical theme. Sure enough, loneliness / a fear of being alone / dissatisfaction came out on top, accounting for around a third of all the songs. Sex came second; descriptions of being in love and the catchall 'other' were joint third and novelty songs last. Try it for yourself . . . Recall some popular hits and think about the emotional state they describe. Of course there are plenty of exceptions, but it's striking how many say something essentially similar to the memorable refrain of Radiohead's breakthrough hit 'Creep': 'I don't belong here.'

It seems we've grown apart – not only from nature, but from each other and even a meaningful sense of ourselves. The songs describe feelings of alienation. By describing them, they reassure us that we are not the only one with those feelings. At the very least, this consoles us making our days more bearable – music helps us endure alienation. But at its best, music can prise open the cracks that let in the light, to paraphrase Leonard Cohen, illuminating the path to a better world. By reminding us how good it feels to emotionally connect with others, it invites us to imagine a less alienated future. For the Austrian writer Ernst Fischer, all art expresses a longing for a sense of unity that we've somehow lost. It enables us to locate our very personal and subjective feelings within a kind of shared collective consciousness.

Of course, you have to be able to imagine a future to imagine a less alienated one. When I listen to some of the music to have emerged in the twenty-first century – particularly new electronic dance music – I hear fragmentation, chaos and nihilism. Is this the sound of people giving up on their futures; turning their backs on society, or at least the possibility of changing it? Take US dubstep legend Skrillex. If you've never heard his music, think retro gaming arcade meets war zone. Bleeps, sirens and shards of synth chords divide and subdivide over a breakbeat and the gargantuan 'wub' of wobble bass. Lyrics are few and the meaning ambiguous. Is this a musical representation of the barrage of information and stimuli we are subjected to in an increasingly online and atomised world? Don't get me wrong – I'm a fan – the music is brimming with originality and energy. Many a time I've stretched the goodwill of my neighbours with my inability to resist turning up 'Bangerang'. But the experience is not like listening to say, bebop – it doesn't invite us to engage intellectually with the creative journeys of musicians. Nor does it feel sensuous in the same way a lot of classic dance music does – it's not an invocation to some sort of sexual communion on the dance floor. Instead euphoria comes from unquestion-ingly surrendering to the sonic assault and bouncing with abandon to that breakbeat and bass.

At their best, overtly political acts like Public Enemy or Rage Against The Machine evoked a spirit of rebellion and locked lyrical crosshairs on those who needed to be rebelled against. Skrillex, by contrast, delivers a visceral sonic assault seemingly devoid of social critique. Is the Machine winning? Is this music for people who find it easier to imagine the end of the world than systemic change – people resigned to 'living in the end times', as the maverick philosopher Slavoj Žižek put it? 'We're doomed anyway, so why not party hard!?' Perhaps. Whether politically ambiguous new music helps to awake the inner revolutionary or the inner nihilist will be determined by the context we create for it. Partly it will hinge on whether people – young people in particular – feel a sense of possibility and hope.

If much of our favourite music describes and consoles our feelings of alienation, then gigs offer us temporary escape from them. They provide us with a chance to jump, dance and sing together in a collective expression of joy. This is also true of nightclubs, house parties, street sound systems and other get-togethers where music is played. But gigs offer the added excitement of the spectacle of music being made live. A conversation I once had with a seasoned performer got me thinking about why live music is so appealing to witness. He told me his job was to make the audience wish they could be like him while they're at work on Monday morning. At first I wasn't sure what he meant. But then I started reflecting on the fact that in contrast to most workers, performers seem to express themselves through their work. They appear to combine their physical, intellectual and creative attributes – even their soul – in a tangible, immediate act of production. They present us with the tantalising mirage of un-alienated labour – work that is actually deeply satisfying – and leave us enviously speculating about their glamorous lives. After all, what may be a highlight of the summer for the audience, appears to be the everyday lived reality of the touring musician. What could be more intriguing and attractive than that?

The truth, of course, is more complicated. I know all too well that musicians face many of the same frustrations and fears as every other worker. On the question of alienation, those of us who tour are actually more removed from the collective – in some senses more alienated – than most. We may bring people together, but we do so as itinerants removed from society and placed in a bubble of tour-buses, hotels, dressing rooms and VIP areas. As the ever pessimistic Adorno once remarked:

> The practise of music is historically linked with the idea of selling one's talent, and even one's self, directly, without intermediaries, rather than selling one's labour in congealed form, as a commodity; and through the

ages the musician, like the actor, has been closely akin to the lackey, the jester, or the prostitute. Although musical performance presupposes the most exacting labour, the fact that the artist appears in person, and the coincidence between his existence and his achievement, together create the illusion that he does it for fun, that he earns his living without honest labour, and this very illusion is readily exploited.[5]

This might make difficult reading for musicians – not to mention actors, comics and sex workers – but there's no doubt that the illusion of un-alienated labour is encouraged by the music industry. We musicians are paid not just to play, but also to perform – to act as if we are emotionally connected to the music and moment whether or not we really feel it. The idea that we're 'living the dream' sells. It also makes our work highly sought-after, helping to drive down wages and terms of employment. In my corner of the industry, life is certainly pretty precarious. Despite many of us being Musicians' Union members, we are usually expected to go to work on the basis of verbal agreements that can be rescinded at any time without compensation. I have never received sick pay or holiday pay and I've sometimes had to chase fees owing to me for months on end. Some I've simply given up on. And the fees are far lower than many people assume. We may rock out next to famous millionaires, but paying the rent is sometimes a struggle. The stresses associated with this sort of working life are reflected in the frequency with which drugs and alcohol are misused in the industry.

US government statistics recently revealed that 11.5 per cent of adults working in the 'arts, entertainment and recreation' sector report heavy drinking in the last month. That's above all the other sectors except 'accommodation and food services' (11.8 per cent), construction (16.5 per cent) and mining (17.5 per cent).[6] I suspect that if our category was narrowed to 'touring musicians and crew', we would top the chart. Those stresses also help to explain why so many musicians are enticed into the ranks of the military. The British Army is the largest employer of musicians in the UK – a fact that underlines the importance ascribed to music by the state. Its recruitment literature boasts: 'As an Army Musician you get many benefits that you'd never have as a civilian musician. You get regular pay and job security.'

Musicians are not freed from alienation or exploitation at all. But our work does provide a spectacle that moves people and helps them to feel emotionally connected. This is part of the reason why gigs remain so popular. It also explains the huge popularity of music festivals – if a gig feels good, lots of gigs presented alongside loads of other cool stuff feels fantastic. At their best, festivals offer a tantalising glimpse of a less inhibited and more caring way to relate to one another. They can leave punters and performers alike with a lingering sense that our everyday lives could and should be better. They invite us to believe that another world is possible.

Pyramid Stage

Three hours and counting. Queue up at catering. Find myself next to Nora Jones. She looks more, well . . . *ordinary* than I imagined – and lovelier – not at all affected by her stardom. The food is excellent – loads of great veggie salads, apple pie with ice-cream (my favourite).

One hour and counting. Back to the dressing room to play some guitar. Major scales in thirds, chromatic shapes up and down the neck – strict alternate picking. That kooky C major to G7/B combination picking thing I learned from Jim Campilongo. Then some rest . . . move a bag parked on a dressing-room sofa (why do people always do that?) and slump for a while.

Forty minutes and counting. Carefully iron my shirt and change into stage clothes. Return guitar to Nobby, my guitar tech.

Twenty minutes and counting. Start the stretching regime I learned once in a capoeira class – slowly limbering up every part of the body from head to toes.

Ten minutes and counting. Collect radio pack and in-ear monitors. Fix pack to belt, run the lead down inside my shirt, plug into the pack and drape the 'ears' over my own.

Seven minutes and counting. Chew on an energy sweet. Politely refuse Maxi's offer of some protein-heavy energy drink, but accept a plastic cup with a splash of Laurent-Perrier rosé champagne. Don't really want any, but take a sip to show team spirit.

Five minutes and counting. Follow tour manager along bouncy flooring, past a large group of musos and industry slickers hoping to meet Stevie Wonder, up some scaffolding steps to the back of the stage. Insert 'ears' and click radio pack on, listen for feed from ambient mics. It's there.

One minute and counting. Peek at the crowd, check the position of my amp and effects pedal board. Bounce up and down a bit, shadow box, stretch, hug the other band members, focus focus focus . . . and go.

Glastonbury's Pyramid stage. Faithless are playing the penultimate slot (before Stevie Wonder) on Sunday night. For nearly two decades, I've been a devoted punter and regular (smaller stage) performer at this extraordinary festival. With the sun slowly setting behind a crowd of about 80,000 people, I quickly clock the fact that this moment must be the leading contender for all-time-career-high-point. Who'd have thought it!

A few hours later, I'm flying high, joyfully pogoing to heavy drum and bass with some close friends at Arcadia – the giant fire-spewing mechanical spider / DJ's crow's nest. My post-gig booze-addled thoughts return to the image of that Pyramid stage crowd and some long held questions . . . Where does all this incredible collective euphoria come from? Why does it feel so good to get together in this way? And why have festivals grown in popularity over the past few decades? Why did underground raves explode into the mainstream global electronic dance music scene we see today? Has our desire to escape our everyday lives – to glimpse a different way of being – intensified? If so why? . . . Is alienation getting worse? What do these things say about our stage of development – our 'social moment'?

Unsurprisingly, answers weren't forthcoming that night. In fact, it's not until my conversation with Barry in Trinidad a few years later that something starts to crystallise in my mind. Carnival, I had discovered, can only be understood by looking back at the political struggles of the nineteenth century. Perhaps an understanding of my experiences also requires some historical perspective. The growth in popularity of both music festivals and electronic dance music has roughly coincided with the rise of an economic model called neoliberalism. Is that mere coincidence? Maybe an understanding of what neoliberalism is – how it has affected communities and changed attitudes – can help us get a grip on why people find pleasure where they do. The following chapter is my attempt at a brief musical history of neoliberalism.

CHAPTER SIX

A Short Musical History of Neoliberalism

We've seen how the most popular songs of the twentieth century reveal a creeping sense of alienation, but there's no doubt the middle of the century was a time of hope for millions around the world. Colonialism was crumbling, workers' wages rising and cracks were starting to appear in the USSR with the death of Stalin in 1954 and the Hungarian uprising of 1956. Campaigns for racial, sexual and gender equality gained ground in the USA and left-wing movements won popular support across the Caribbean and Latin America. In May 1968, Paris became the centre of a near revolution that inspired a generation into radical politics. The ruling classes were worried. They decided to try to reverse the tide, tighten their grip on society and find a way of extracting higher profits from workers for lower pay. A strategy was drawn up by the Chicago School of economists who advocated the complete deregulation of the market and removal of any obstacles to that end. The test ground was Chile and the first obstacles were a democratically elected left-leaning president, Salvador Allende, and a massive radical workers' movement. The strategists solution was a CIA orchestrated coup that took place on 11 September 1973, costing the lives of more than 10,000 Chileans including the president. It was here in the destruction of democracy that capitalism's most recent incarnation – neoliberalism – was born.

One of the victims of the Chilean coup was the singer/ songwriter, poet and theatre director Victor Jara. A supporter of the elected president's Popular Unity party, Jara pioneered a new folk-influenced form of politicised music known as Nueva Canción Chilena (New Chilean Song). The American political folk singer Phil Ochs told his brother after meeting Jara: 'I just met the real thing. Pete Seeger and I are nothing compared to this. I mean here's a man who really is what he's saying.'[1] Following the coup, Jara was arrested, taken to Chile Stadium and tortured before being shot in the head. Around 3,000 other workers, students, trade unionists and activists were also massacred in the stadium.

This wasn't the first example of a political singer being executed, but it was the first to reach the consciousness of a generation of North Americans and Europeans. The coup sent a shockwave around the world. Liberals who had previously thought radical change could be peacefully ushered in through the ballot box learned a bitter lesson: when the ruling classes fail to win consent, they resort to ruthless coercion to achieve their aims. Jara had understood this for some time. After being physically attacked by right-wing thugs at a university gig in 1969, his wife Joan noted:

It made Victor realise very clearly just what he might expect if he continued to express in his songs what he felt had to be said. But there is no doubt that his commitment and his resolve were strengthened rather than weakened by it. He took a step forwards rather than backwards in the face of violence, taking the risk with his eyes open.[2]

Jara's eyes were also open to the covert battle to manufacture consent. He could see beyond the immediate threat of fascism and understood the more subtle ways in which people are manipulated. Protest singers and their songs, he realised, were well within the reach of rulers' attempts to control culture:

US imperialism understands very well the magic of communication through music and persists in filling our young people with all sorts of commercial tripe. With professional expertise they have taken certain measures: first the commercialisation of so called 'protest music'; second, the creation of 'idols' of protest music who obey the same rules and suffer from the same constraints as the other idols of the consumer music industry – they last a little while and then disappear. Meanwhile they are useful in neutralising the innate spirit of rebellion of young people. The term 'protest song' is no longer valid because it is ambiguous and has been misused. I prefer the term 'revolutionary song'.[3]

Rock Against Racism

The Chilean coup was a brutal and audacious escalation of a global assault by the political right. The neoliberal project sought to roll back progressive movements, enabling the rich to become richer while others suffered. In 1957, Britons were told by Prime Minister Harold Macmillan that they had 'never had it so good'. Many would have agreed. But in 1976 the International Monetary Fund insisted that James Callaghan's Labour government force through deep public spending cuts. As unemployment rose, working-class youths looked for ways to express the new mood of betrayal and anger. Hippie psychedelia and bombastic progressive rock were ditched by a generation determined to reclaim music as a vehicle for the direct, visceral expression of working-class rebellion. As DJ and filmmaker Don Letts explained:

In late-70s London the political, social and economic climate was pretty bad. My white mates were very pissed-off. I was already pissed-off because I was first generation black and British and had plenty to be pissed-off about. Fortunately for me I had a soundtrack to ease my pain – that was reggae music. My white mates never had that – the popular music of the time was like stadium rock (over-indulgent shit with twenty-minute solos) and it didn't reflect the feeling on the street. So my white friends set about creating their own soundtrack: of the people; for the people; by the people. That became punk rock.[4]

But while Letts and his friends mixed at trendy London venues like the Roxy, other punks flirted dangerously with symbols of the far right, including the swastika. This was at a time when the ruling class was trying to divide communities by blaming immigrants for economic hardships and social unrest. Shamefully, white British blues musician Eric Clapton fell for the old trick. While drunk onstage at the Birmingham Odeon, he declared his support for right-wing Tory MP Enoch Powell, adding 'I think we should send 'em all back' and that Britain was in danger of becoming 'a black colony'. The hypocrisy was breath-taking – Clapton's whole career had been based on appropriating black music and he had just had a hit with a cover version of Bob Marley's 'I Shot the Sheriff'. Not for the first or last time, the organised far left played a decisive role in combating a dangerous lurch to the right. One of their key weapons was music, in particular punk rock and reggae.

Red Saunders, a photographer, music fan and political activist, described the shock and disgust felt by many at Clapton's outburst: 'This was when David Bowie was prattling on about Hitler being 'the first superstar' and Rod Stewart decided Britain was too overcrowded for him. It just made me sick with disappointment, but then fucking pissed off.'[5] Saunders and some friends responded with a letter published in the *New Musical Express*, *Melody Maker*, *Sounds* and the *Socialist Worker*. They wrote:

> Come on Eric . . . Own up – half your music is black. You are rock music's biggest colonist . . . You've got to fight the racist poison otherwise you degenerate into the sewer with the rats and all the money men who ripped off rock culture with their cheque books and plastic crap. We want to organise a rank and file movement against the racist poison in music . . . We urge support for Rock Against Racism. P.S. Who shot the Sheriff, Eric? It sure as hell wasn't you!

Within a fortnight there were more than 600 replies with many bands offering to perform for the cause. Three months later, in November 1976, Rock Against Racism (RAR) held its first ever gig at a pub in East London. On 30 April 1978, the grassroots movement succeed in bringing more than 80,000 people together for a march from Trafalgar Square to east London's Victoria

Park, where the Tom Robinson Band, the Clash, Steel Pulse, X-Ray Spex, Buzzcocks, the Ruts, Sham 69 and Generation X performed. The procession was led by the Southall-based reggae band Misty in Roots, who played from the back of a lorry. A second march and gig in Brixton's Brockwell Park drew even larger numbers and featured Stiff Little Fingers, Aswad and Elvis Costello. 35,000 attended a RAR carnival in Manchester, 8,000 in Edinburgh and 5,000 in both Southampton and Cardiff.

The big names at the big events mattered, but what was most effective about RAR was that it encouraged people to organise gigs in their own communities. Several hundred took place up and down the country and the RAR fanzine *Temporary Hoarding* was distributed to thousands. The emphasis on grassroots self-organisation was very effective. I was just a child at the time, but I have a very clear memory that although racism was commonplace, it was *not* cool. The cool kids were anti-racist and many were into reggae. I have no doubt that this and the decline of the racist National Front at the end of the 1970s was due in significant part to RAR, its sister organisation the Anti-Nazi League, and the Socialist Workers Party, who provided leadership, organisational muscle and resources. At a time when high-profile politicians, sections of the mainstream media, and some celebrities were telling us to fear immigration and reject multiculturalism, RAR successfully helped to steer the 'common sense' of a generation towards anti-racism. One

RAR founding member, David Widgery, summed it up: '[RAR] cured the schizophrenia between Marxist politics and modern culture ... Black music was our catechism ... our experience had taught us a golden political rule: how people find their pleasure, entertainment and celebration is also how they find their sexual identity, their political courage and their strength to change.'[6]

The British far left may have provided the world with a model of how music can be used in the battle against racism, but the neoliberal politics that contributed to the problem in the first place continued to be aggressively rolled out. US President Ronald Reagan cut services to poor Americans while secretly funding death-squads to destabilise left-wing movements in Latin America. In Britain, Prime Minister Margaret Thatcher declared war on the trade unions and went about privatising publicly-owned utilities.

In the US, victims of the onslaught found a voice in a new culture emerging from the poor black neighbourhoods of New York City. One of hip-hop's first international hits, 'The Message', by Grandmaster Flash and the Furious Five, was no less damning in its assessment of the plight of poor African Americans than 'Strange Fruit' had been nearly half a century before. It describes the misery of life in the ghetto with the story of a child who is used, abused and ultimately found hung dead in a cell.

In early 1980s Britain, unemployment rocketed and riots broke out across the country. The song 'Ghost

Town', penned by Jerry Dammers and performed by the Specials, captured the scenes of desolation and feelings of anger experienced in working-class communities. It topped the charts as inner cities burned.

Artists Against Apartheid and Solidarność

Despite these hardships, many Britons still found ways to express solidarity with those who had it worse elsewhere in the world. Thatcher's government had branded Nelson Mandela and the ANC 'terrorists', but more and more people supported their cause. In 1984, the Special AKA's 'Free Nelson Mandela' reached number 9 in the UK charts. Dammers also supported the call from South Africans to impose a boycott on the country, but it was the American guitarist Steve Van Zandt, best known for his work with Bruce Springsteen and his later acting role in *The Sopranos*, who penned the boycott anthem. Featuring a stellar line-up of artists including Bob Dylan, Bruce Springsteen, Miles Davis, U2 and Keith Richards, among many others, 'Sun City' was released in 1985 under the name Artists United Against Apartheid. Despite resistance from radio, it achieved moderate success with Top 40 chart positions in the US, UK, Canada and Australia. The song's lyrics implored artists to stay away from apartheid South Africa. Its title came from a notorious luxury resort just outside of Johannesburg – a kind of mini Las Vegas a stone's throw from the impoverished Soweto township. Some British and American musicians ignored the call. Few would defend their decision now, but opinions are more divided about Paul Simon's breach of the boycott to work with black South African musicians on his *Graceland* album (1986). Fans point out that it launched the international careers of several black South African musicians and introduced a global audience to the country's many musical riches – a contribution that reverberated long after the fall of apartheid. My own view is that *Graceland* was perhaps the greatest album that never should have been. The wishes of the majority of South Africans, as articulated by their jailed and exiled leaders, must surely take precedence over the existence of another Paul Simon album, however good.

It's hard to assess what contribution the cultural boycott made to the struggle. Certainly, the most important challenges to the apartheid regime came from within the country – particularly the wave of strikes and demonstrations held by black workers throughout the 1980s. But the international solidarity movement did raise awareness about the crimes of apartheid. It created a climate in which large companies did start to dis-invest from the country, significantly impacting the economy. Boycott remains one of the most contentious tactics in the realm of culture and politics – it's a question I'll return to.

Within South Africa, music also played a critical role. It is well known that the huge political rallies and demonstrations were animated with song, dance and chants. Secret concerts and smuggled recordings of banned black musicians also gave fuel to the fires of mass resistance. Almost every musical genre was utilised. The contribution made by jazz and popular musicians including Hugh Masekela, the Mahotella Queens, Miriam Makeba, Abdullah Ibrahim and others is well documented. Punk also played its part. The bands who had Rocked Against Racism in London's parks inspired a generation of angry young South Africans who formed bands such as Durban's Wild Youth, the all-female Leopard, Screaming Foetus, Power Age, Johannesburg's multiracial National Wake and Cape Town's Kalahari Surfers.

As well as taking inspiration from the anti-racist scene in Britain, some South African punks also looked to revolutionary movements growing in opposition to the Stalinist regimes of Eastern Europe. Johannesburg-based, Afrikaans speaking, multiracial band Koos cite Polish Theatre and the underground bands of Czechoslovakia as influences. Durban's Power Age and the Gay Marines set up benefit gigs in solidarity with the Polish worker's movement *Solidarność* (Solidarity). The connection may not seem obvious, but the struggles against totalitarian states in Eastern Europe and apartheid in South Africa represented two key fronts in the battle for a better world in the 1980s. Both would achieve significant success by the end of the decade. The Berlin Wall fell in 1989, accelerating the collapse of regimes in the region and Nelson Mandela was released in 1990. By 1994 he was South Africa's president.

The political and ideological onslaught of neoliberalism continued to have a huge impact across the world in the 1980s. Some were persuaded that this was an exciting new age of individual freedom. The emergence of 'young upwardly-mobile professionals', or 'yuppies', in North America and Britain was cited as evidence that untold riches could be yours if you were entrepreneurial and willing to work hard. But in poorer communities, people became increasingly disillusioned. As Nelson George noted of hip-hop music from the era:

> Rap records said quite explicitly that life for so many young black Americans had nothing to do with Harvard T-shirts and sorority pins. The gap between street-corner culture and middle-class comfort had never seemed so large in postwar America because, unlike young blacks twenty years before, b-boys rarely connected to concepts like 'hope' and 'I have a Dream'. The optimism of the 1960s was not even a memory for the kids purchasing rap records.[7]

Political leaders did little to win back consent. They simply repeated a new mantra: 'There Is No Alternative'. Notice the stark contrast to Macmillan's 'You've never had it so good'. In an attempt to find some moral cover for their ongoing attacks on the livelihoods of working people, the right-wing politicians and their supporters selectively quoted from *The Wealth of Nations*, written in 1776 by the eccentric Enlightenment economist Adam Smith. Smith argued that the 'invisible hand of the market' would naturally guide wealth from the pockets of the rich into the hands of the poor, so raising the material wealth of the whole of society. In the 1980s, this idea was called the 'trickle-down effect'. But Smith got it wrong. As early as 1867, Karl Marx argued in his classic *Capital* that Smith's reasoning was flawed and that the logic of the market would actually lead to an increasing gap between rich and poor. That is precisely what happened in the 1980s, both within wealthy countries such as the US and Britain and between different economies around the world. For the most part, wealth was not trickling down, it was being sucked upwards.

By the time Thatcher won a third term in office, poor Britons knew the trickle-down would never come. She needed a new soundbite to fend off the critics and rally the faithful. It was unleashed in 1987 in an interview for a women's magazine:

I think we have gone through a period when too many children and people have been given to understand 'I have a problem, it is the Government's job to cope with it!' or 'I have a problem, I will go and get a grant to cope with it!' 'I am homeless, the Government must house me!' and so they are casting their problems on society and who is society? There is no such thing![8]

The message behind the 'no such thing as society' phrase was clear: the poor only had themselves to blame and didn't deserve any help. Many Britons agreed that this 'tough love' was the only road to modernisation and reform. Others saw that such claims thinly veiled a brutal vision of a dog-eat-dog world. With the trade union movement cowed by Thatcher's key victories against the miners and print workers, those who rejected her vision struggled to find an effective political voice. But they did express their desire for a more caring sense of community through culture, and in particular music.

Rave New World

Music has always been used to bring people together and enhance a sense of community. Contemporary dance music has its roots in conscious attempts to do precisely that by groups excluded from mainstream society. In the 1970s and '80s, new music emerged from the black lesbian, gay, bisexual and transgender underground of a decaying New York City and the industrial cities of Chicago and Detroit. People who faced social exclusion due to prejudice – in particular racism, homophobia and transphobia – were putting music at the centre of an attempt to create an alternative sense of community. Luis-Manuel Garcia described the genesis of the scene:

> In New York City at the beginning of the 1970s, queers of colour (primarily of African American and Latin-Caribbean ancestry) and many straight-but-not-narrow allies came together to create small pockets of space in the city's harsh urban landscape – spaces where they could be safe, be themselves, be someone else for a while, and be with others in ways not permitted in the 'normal' everyday world. Music was an essential part of these gatherings, and the sound of these events would eventually develop into the style called disco.[9]

The desire to create a sense of community was consciously political from the start, as legendary record producer Nile Rodgers described:

> I'd say [the disco pioneers] were even more expressive, political, communal than the hippies before them, because they bonded through their bodies, through dance; they were propelled by a new kind of funky groove music. Dance had become primal and ubiquitous, a powerful communication tool, every bit as motivational as an Angela Davis speech or treasured as that eighteen-dollar, three-day Woodstock Festival ticket.[10]

By the late 1970s, disco had exploded into the mainstream, but for bigots its roots were all too evident. Steve Dahl, a Chicago-based 'shock jock', spearheaded a 'Disco Sucks' movement complete with a vigilante mob recruited from listeners. After staging several unruly anti-disco club events, Dahl issued the call for a 'Disco Demolition Night' at which disco records would be blown up in a baseball stadium during the interval between two games. At least 50,000 people packed into Chicago's Comiskey Park to take part in the bizarre hate fest, which turned into a near riot. Though it was by far the biggest event pulled off by the Disco Sucks campaign, the demolition night was not an isolated incident. The outpouring of bigoted rage shook the mainstream music industry. Nile Rodgers described how by 1979:

> The Disco Sucks movement and its backlash were so toxic, people in the industry – people who were eating off the record sales coming from dance music – were all too afraid to be associated with anything disco . . . What I saw was classic hypocrisy: people who'd been making a fortune off this music willingly throwing it under a bus, rather than standing up for it when it became uncomfortable or politically inconvenient. To put it another way, they milked it when it was up and kicked it when it was down.[11]

Disco recording artists and fans watched in dazed disbelief as dance-floors were deserted and mirror balls mothballed across America. However, the shock-jocks and their explosives did nothing to abate the basic desire for community. In countries such as the UK, rising unemployment and falling public spending were starting to shatter lives in working-class neighbourhoods. People needed some good times and hugs like never before. The belief that music might help soon gained currency. By the late 1980s, disco's musical protégés, house and techno, were seized upon by young working-class people – precisely those who had been told by Thatcher that there was no such thing as society. Massive, illegal house music parties, or raves, became the fastest growing underground scene in the late days of Thatcher's Britain. In a rejection of her dog-eat-dog social order, young Britons created their own summers of love in 1988 and 1989.

Just like the San Francisco scene of two decades earlier from which they took the name, the summers of love and the underground rave scene they spawned were wrought with contradictions. For many ravers they did indeed provide powerful – if temporary and drug fuelled – feelings of love, freedom, community and belonging. For many of the club owners, drug dealers and other associated entrepreneurs, they were cash cows to be miked dry. These contradictions were symptomatic of a widely-held desire to break down alienation in an age when traditional forms of oppositional politics seemed to have failed. The emphasis was on temporary escape from the 'real' world, not attempts to change it. But still, the spectacle of thousands of predominantly working-class young people communicating through covert networks of flyers and phone trees and congregating in unsanctioned places – often the country estates of the old landed rich – worried the government. Their response was a draconian piece of legislation called the Criminal Justice Act which came into law in 1994. Section 5 specified:

> This section applies to a gathering on land in the open air of 100 or more persons (whether or not trespassers) at which amplified music is played during the night (with or without intermissions) and is such as, by reason of its loudness and duration and the time at which it is played, is likely to cause serious distress to the inhabitants of the locality; and for this purpose—
>
> (a) such a gathering continues during intermissions in the music and, where the gathering extends over several days, throughout the period during which amplified music is played at night (with or without intermissions); and
>
> (b) 'music' includes sounds wholly or predominantly characterised by the emission of a succession of repetitive beats.[12]

Repetitive beats. In his book *Jazz – A People's Music* (1948), Sydney Finkelstein cautions those critics who heard African drumming in the rhythms of jazz. He pointed out that aside from deliberate African references in the playing of virtuosic drummers such as Max Roach, jazz was all-American. Jazz rhythms, syncopation and swing spoke of an optimistic new age of individual expression and creativity. They create a free and fluid space in which soloists are spurred on in their musical travels. Traditional African drumming, by contrast, has its roots in ceremony and community – the interlocking rhythms drawing people together as a collective. Soloists still momentarily take flight, but return to the solid foundations of home. In the Jazz Age, liberation meant freedom to express oneself as an individual, uninhibited by old-fashioned values and prejudices. But by the 1990s, though the fight for equality was far from won, individualism had come to represent an uncaring dog-eat-dog mentality. Though they are further separated by time, timbre and technology, perhaps the repetitive beats of house music have more in common with traditional African drumming than jazz ever did. They speak not of individual virtuosity but a shared desire to melt and merge trance-like into the collective. This was music offering a temporary path back to unity for those who found in the promised land of individualism only decaying communities, dead-end jobs and dole queues.

For some of those involved in the early days of rave, the scene became a lifestyle. Luton's 'Exodus Collective' and others created permanent communes while nomadic sound systems such as Spiral Tribe set off in convoys across Europe to meet comrades in techno around the continent. What they shared was a belief that partying should change the world, or at least their own lives. An array of anti-capitalist and anarchist ideas were discussed and lived out in ageing coaches, caravans, communes and amid huge sound systems hastily erected in moonlit fields. But the majority of ravers were weekenders who would share tales of ecstasy and excess around the office watercooler on a Monday morning as the come-down kicked in. For most, the campaign against the attempt to criminalise the scene was about as directly political as things got. An almost medieval echo of commoners versus landowners did contribute to feelings of class consciousness, but the aim remained hedonistic escape from the drudgery of the working week or the monotony of life on the dole. Despite changes in government, neoliberal economic policies lived on throughout the 1990s and were adopted by all the mainstream political parties. House music lived on too – also increasingly in the mainstream. The illegal free raves and ideals of community gave way to expensive super-clubs, high-earning celebrity DJs, VIP areas and the rest. A journalist travelling with Spiral Tribe in the mid-1990s acknowledged that a meeting of sound systems somewhere in the fields of rural France known as a 'Teknival' represented: '...a last stand against the forces of commerce which had transformed the rave dream into a corporate-sponsored fantasy, against the military-industrial-entertainment complex which had, yet again, turned rebellion into money'.[13]

In contrast to 'Strange Fruit', 'Free Nelson Mandela' and the punks who Rocked Against Racism, rave was a cultural uprising without a significant political organisation or movement to align itself with. As a result, it was vulnerable to co-option by the very system that its early devotees were trying to escape. The Culture Industry's profiteers performed a jujitsu-style move of their own. The widely-held desire for unity that had given birth to rave was successfully channelled into money-spinning ventures that offered less and less to more and more.

Ultimately the world changed house music, rather than the reverse. But despite the change, something essential remains. This, I believe, is the source of all that euphoria I have witnessed. Music and music events help to console and abate our feelings of alienation. With the spread and impact of neoliberalism, this became increasingly important to growing numbers. Electronic dance music now has a global audience of millions and festivals have boomed precisely because they still offer respite – albeit temporary and corporate branded – from those feelings of atomisation, dislocation and boredom. Narrow ambitions and cut-throat competition characterise workplace culture in a neoliberal world. Dance music and festivals represent an implicit but widely-held desire to explore other ways of being. For all the contradictions of commercialisation, they remain an expression of our desire to come together – not to cheer a national team, wave flags, take sides, worship gods or kings – but to dance, embrace and celebrate each other.

CHAPTER SEVEN

Star Gazing

The more I thought about the story of dance music, the more I noticed a pattern repeated elsewhere. Music often comes from and enhances feelings of community. But it is also frequently co-opted by wealthy elites with quite different interests. Throughout history, rulers have tended to promote music that invites us not to celebrate each other, but the great leader – be that god / the king / a dictator / a 'star' – or a new product. In glorifying its subject, the music emphasises the difference between subject and listener. This seems to be a subtle, but fundamental difference of emphasis between music made *by us for us* (enhancing community) and music commissioned *by them for us* (reinforcing hierarchy).

The distinction doesn't have its origins with Simon Cowell, the postwar advertising industry, or even the twentieth-century dictators discussed earlier. It's as old as class society. Take the example of medieval Europe, where the establishment was composed of feudal lords and the Catholic Church. They were worried that popular songs and dances enjoyed by ordinary people might lead to social unrest. So, in an attempt to steer the masses away from worldly pleasures and towards spiritual contemplation, church authorities placed restrictions on music. Repetitive beats were not yet a problem, but they did forbid the use of certain musical note combinations or *intervals*. The most difficult sounding, or 'dissonant' interval, the flat fifth, or tritone, was branded *diabolus in musica* (the devil in music) and even the sweet-sounding bedrock of Western harmony, the major third, remained banned in churches for nearly two centuries. In the same way that 1950s conservatives feared the influence of rock and roll, so in the 1150s, music that strayed from plainly sung octaves, fourths and fifths was considered morally corrupting and a threat to the social order.

Notre Dame cathedral in Paris was the centre for establishment music at the time. Despite the restrictions, important musical innovation did take place there – the practice of organum, or early harmony, developed by Leonin and Perotin, was a revelation. But far from the splendours of Paris a different sound was heard – voices singing together an interval of a third apart and moving in parallel. Soon the whole of Europe swooned to the sound of the taboo interval. Parallel thirds dominated popular songs and duets for instruments such as the lur – a metal horn that became widespread following improvements in the working of copper. This was the rock 'n' roll, hip-hop, rave or grime of its time – loved by the people, loathed by their rulers. *They* wanted music to help us gaze upward in spiritual contemplation. *We* wanted music to help us get down and dirty.

The musical standoff between the establishment and the people lasted nearly 200 years until famine ravaged the continent with plague in its wake. Bitterness and resentments flared up as never before. In 1325, the peasants of western Flanders took up arms, refusing to pay any dues to the feudal lords or church. They were only defeated when the king of France intervened in 1328. In 1358 another rural uprising exploded, this time in the Seine valley of northern France. Nobles were attacked and chateaux burnt to the ground.[1] With the growing threat from below, rulers became desperate to reinforce the message that the social order is ordained by God – attempts to change it were both futile and blasphemous. But this was a pill too bitter for the rebellious masses to swallow. Reluctantly, church authorities agreed to sweeten it by finally accepting popular innovations including those in musical harmony. This was the start of the European Renaissance. Fundamentally, the Church's message hadn't changed, but with musical restrictions lifted, at least their tunes were catchier. The new permissive attitude set the stage for Guillaume de Machaut (c.1300–77) – considered by many to be the West's first great composer – and the whole canon of Western classical music that followed.

In the intervening centuries, the world and its music have been utterly transformed. But we continue to live in societies divided by class, and rulers remain as keen as ever that we gaze upwards in awe. I'm not referring to the sizeable market for religious music, significant as that is. I'm thinking about the way the music industry makes every effort to create 'stars'.

Musical stars, in the modern sense, first emerged with the rise of the bourgeoisie in the wake of the French Revolution (1789–91). It seems the new class wanted their own brash ambition, spirit of adventure and lust for power to be mirrored in music. The virtuosic Italian violinist Nicolò Paganini fitted the bill perfectly. Born in Genoa in 1782, Paganini made his public debut at the age of nine and was on his way to becoming a legend by the early 1800s. Dressed entirely in black, his appearance was cadaverous – the original skinny goth. He did nothing to dispel rumours of a pact with the devil, which in this new age simply added to the promotional hype. Sell out tours of Europe earned him a fortune, but he still had to occasionally pawn his violins to pay off gambling debts. Curtis W. Davis explained his appeal in the new age:

With the rapid growth of cities, the soloist stood out as a potential individual hero, an ideal towards which the revolutionary progressive spirit of the age could aspire. The soloist could also cater more effectively to a greater number, in halls holding two thousand or more. The aristocracy may have been the first to fill these halls, but the bankers, lawyers and merchants were not far behind.[2]

From the stalls of concert halls across Europe, bankers, lawyers and merchants cultivated the view that society should no longer bow to throne and altar, but to individual ambition and success. The musical heights scaled by Paganini were achieved by his own hard work. The economic heights enjoyed by the class who made up much of his audience, by contrast, were the result of a new system of exploiting the labour of others. The shackles of feudalism had largely been cast off, clearing the way for the bourgeoisie to organise labour in new, more productive ways. What emerged, first in Britain and then across Europe and beyond, was a system of industrial capitalism that would reshape the world.

Whatever your position in society, the early days of industrial capitalism were uncertain, exhilarating and sometimes terrifying. Music became correspondingly pulse-raising. Paganini spurred composers such as Berlioz and Chopin to new heights and flights of individual expression. He also inspired Franz Liszt – the most important musical innovator of the age. Liszt too had rock star qualities, delightfully described by Frederich Engels in a letter to his sister dated 16 April 1842:

Mr. Liszt has been here and enchanted all the ladies by his piano playing. The Berlin ladies were so besotted by him that there was a free fight during one of his concerts for possession of a glove which he had dropped, and two sisters are now enemies for life because one of them snatched the glove from the other. Countess Schlippenbach poured the tea which the great Liszt had left in a cup into her Eau-de-Cologne bottle after she had poured the Eau-de-Cologne on the ground. She has since sealed the bottle and placed it on top of her writing-desk to his eternal memory, and feasts her eyes on it every morning, as can be seen in a cartoon which appeared about it. There never was such a scandal. The young ladies fought over him, but he snubbed them frightfully and preferred to go and drink champagne with a couple of students. There are a couple of pictures of the great, charming, heavenly, genial, divine Liszt in every house. I will draw you a portrait of him.

F. Liszt

By the way, he must have earned at least 10,000 talers here, and his hotel bill amounted to 3,000 talers – apart from what he spent in taverns. I tell you, he's a real man. He drinks twenty cups of coffee a day, two ounces of coffee every cup, and ten bottles of champagne, from which it can fairly safely be concluded that he lives in a kind of perpetual drunken haze ... He has now gone off to Russia, and one wonders whether the ladies there will also go as crazy.[3]

It's telling that Liszt snubbed the adoring bourgeois women, preferring to get drunk with students. It reminds us that although rulers like to bask in the reflected glory of stars, stars don't always want to indulge them. Sometimes that's because they don't agree with what the rulers are doing or what they represent. Sure enough, Liszt's choice of drinking buddies was made against the backdrop of a growing mood of disappointment with the new society. Many poor people forced off the land by 'enclosure acts' had to make their way to cities to find waged work in huge new mills and factories. Conditions were appalling – the English poet William Blake echoed the views of millions when he famously described the mills as 'dark and satanic' in a poem first published in 1808. It may have been Paganini who made a pact with the devil, but it was the new industrialists in the audience who presided over the hellish. Perhaps Liszt's prolific champagne intake can best be understood as his attempt to avoid one

of the worst hangovers in history . . . In the harsh light
of the morning after the bourgeois revolutions, people
were waking up to the grim realities of capitalism. As the
Austrian writer Ernst Fischer described:

> The sincere humanist artist was bound to feel a profound
> disillusionment when faced with the thoroughly
> prosaic, thoroughly sobering, yet disquieting results
> of the bourgeois-democratic revolution . . . [He] could
> no longer affirm such a world. He could no longer
> believe with a clear conscience that the victory of the
> bourgeoisie meant the triumph of humanity.[4]

Composers increasingly explored dark new themes
of death and destiny in their music as working people
organised against exploitation. Popular songs were
one way in which they shared their discontent and set
out demands for better conditions and suffrage. Lyrics
would be printed on sheets known as 'broadsides' that
were circulated widely in working-class communities.
But by the end of the century, new technology extended
the bourgeoisie's control of popular culture. The old
broadsides that had been so cheap and quick to produce
were usurped (along, to a degree, with sheet music) by a
format requiring far more capital investment – the sound
recording.

The first sound recording was made in 1878 on a tinfoil
phonograph. Its inventor, Thomas Edison, enthused

that the talking tinfoil 'will be able to preserve and hear again . . . a memorable speech . . . the last words of a dying man . . . of a distant parent, a lover, a mistress.'[5] Number four on Edison's inventory was the reproduction of music. In truth the scratchy sound quality made it a stretch to include that possibility at all. In 1886, Graham Alexander Bell and his cousin Charles Tainter built a wax cylinder machine with superior sound quality to Edison's tinfoil. The Bell phonograph also had the advantage that its used cylinders could be stored and replayed rather than destroyed, as was the fate of the foil. Wax cylinders were in turn eclipsed by the disc-playing gramophone introduced by Emile Berliner in 1895. The new machine could retail at a fraction of the cost of the wax cylinder models, partly because it offered only half the functionality: it could play music but not record it. Consumers liked the savings and the embryonic recording industry liked the guaranteed market for their pre-recorded discs.

Over the next ten years, sales of disc players and discs grew steadily. The era of the recording star was born. By the first decades of the twentieth century, demand for recordings of popular music boomed in several parts of the world. Music became an industry with growing economic power and part of a mass media that reached huge audiences via the phonograph, radio and cinema. Culture was now big business. Music previously made by working people for their own satisfaction could now be taken by capitalists, packaged and sold back to those people at a profit. There were musical advantages to this new arrangement. For one thing, music could travel and reach new audiences in ways undreamt of before. But with the rise of the mass media and its anointed stars came the consolidation of the bourgeoisie's control of culture. This meant they could not only extract huge profits from audiences – they also had greater leverage over the thoughts in people's heads. The captains of the new music industry skipped over subversive workers' songs that had been popular for decades. Instead, sentimental and patriotic tunes filled the airwaves.

The owners of big business and the mass media have shaped our culture ever since. These days, their efforts to create the rather ephemeral, but clearly very profitable, thing called stardom verge on the ridiculous. After a soundcheck at the MTV awards in Milan, I remember being quickly ushered backstage so that Madonna could take her turn without fear of unsanctioned prying eyes. A camera operator told me they had strict instructions to not zoom in too closely, lest a wrinkle be inadvertently broadcast to the world. Then, after the soundchecks, makeup and wardrobe were complete, all the acts including Madonna were told to file out of a fire exit at the back of the building, past the shabby municipal kitchen and its bins, to a dingy parking lot. Waiting limousines then drove us 50 yards round the corner so we could re-enter the same building by the front door – on a red carpet via shrieking fans and frenzied paparazzi.

Myth: We are 'stars' – or at least extraordinary human beings – whose greatness and glamour are effortless. We don't need to soundcheck and we always look great.

Reality: Though some among us are unimaginably rich, we are ordinary human beings working hard to get the job done. We've been in the venue all afternoon sound-checking. Some of us have wrinkles.

Faithless' frontman, Maxi Jazz, has always had a healthy attitude to the strange myth-making merry-go-round of music marketing. For one thing, he has often repeated his belief that when onstage, we simply hold a mirror up to the audience's own beauty and brilliance. We give them an opportunity to celebrate themselves and each other. His attitude is, if you will, old-school dance music – *by us for us* (enhancing community). But even he has succumbed to requests for ever more messianic promo shots, offers of increasingly expensive designer clothes, his own luxury tour bus and first-class air travel while the majority of the band remain in economy. The industry encourages it. It seems that the more distant and glamorous you appear, and the more cosseted and reliant on managers and aides you become, the more profitable a commodity you are. Stardom probably seems very seductive at first. But according to lots of stars, fame soon feels like a gilded cage. John Lennon remembered the height of the Beatles success as:

. . . complete oppression. I mean we had to go through humiliation upon humiliation with the middle classes and showbiz and the Lord Mayors and all that. They were so condescending and stupid, everybody trying to use us. It was a special humiliation for me because I could never keep my mouth shut and I'd always have to be drunk or pilled to counteract this pressure. It was really hell [. . .] We were all so pressurised that there was hardly any chance of expressing ourselves, especially working at that rate, touring continually and always kept in a cocoon of myths and dreams. It's pretty hard when you are Caesar and everybody is saying how wonderful you are and they are giving you all the goodies and the girls, it's pretty hard to break out of that and say 'Well I don't want to be king, I want to be real.'[6]

I suppose the logic of creating stars, from the industry's point of view, is that people are more likely to part with money if they think they're buying something extraordinary – if they feel it brings them closer to some sort of secular god. Why buy pre-recorded music and expensive concert tickets just to hear an ordinary bloke with a good voice and a few catchy songs – especially if there's one of those in the local bar offering something similar for free? But to bask in the light of a star, to touch the hem of his garment . . . .

Although it's primarily an economic calculation, there's a political side too. As we saw earlier, we love gigs – and especially festivals – because they give us temporary respite from widely-held feelings of alienation. At their best they provide us with a glimpse of a better way to relate to one another and live our lives. But the more the focus is on exceptional individuals rather than collective spirit, the more a new implicit message emerges: stars live extraordinary lives because they are special. The best the rest of us can hope for is an opportunity to enjoy their greatness for a couple of hours at the weekend. The audience is relegated to the role of a sexually frustrated punter at a peep show. They savour a glimpse of the desired object, but end up on the bus home no less frustrated – the gig might have been great, but work on Monday morning is no less unfulfilling and dull. It's hard to measure, but perhaps expectations that it should be otherwise shrink in proportion to the growth of celebrity culture. To paraphrase Oscar Wilde: we're still in the gutter because we're distracted by the stars.

We've arrived back at Adorno's challenging claim that popular music operates on behalf of rulers as a weapon of mass distraction. The powers that be dangle stars above us and we gaze up adoringly. As we swoon over Rihanna's new video, discuss Lady Gaga's latest fashion statement and speculate about Kanye West's mental health, politicians and their corporate clients discreetly get on with kicking us into the gutter. One family,

Walmart heirs, the Waltons, have quietly pocketed more wealth than the bottom 40 per cent of America's citizens combined while refusing to pay their workers a living wage.[7] According to Oxfam, the picture globally is even more grotesque: 62 billionaires own more wealth than the bottom 50 per cent of the world's population.[8] 'Bono will come to your rescue', the billionaires reassure us as they stifle their laughter, neck champagne and sail into the sunset on luxury yachts. Are we whistling the latest Adele hook while Rome burns? Perhaps . . . But just when it seems as if corporations have popular culture in a headlock – just as Adorno's views appear more legitimate than ever before – something happens to remind us that even the most mainstream of mass entertainment remains politically contested . . . .

Beyoncé and Black Lives Matter

In an echo of the 1968 Olympics, it all kicked off with the raising of defiant black fists at a sporting event. This time it wasn't medal-winning athletes on podiums but one of the world's biggest pop stars and her slickly choreographed dancers. At the 2016 NFL Super Bowl 50 performance, in front of a TV audience of over 110 million people, Beyoncé Knowles performed her song 'Formation', making references to the Black Lives Matter campaign, the Black Panthers, Malcolm X and Hurricane Katrina. One of her dancers was also pictured holding a 'Justice 4 Mario Woods' sign (Woods had been shot dead by San Francisco police the previous December). Predictably, Fox News got hot under the collar. Republican former NYC mayor Rudy Giuliani told viewers 'I thought it was really outrageous that she used it as a platform to attack police officers'. There were also reports of some law enforcement organisations calling for a boycott of Beyoncé.

The reaction from other pundits and fans across the mainstream and social media was fascinating. It demonstrated precisely the fault lines we looked at earlier. Some people dismissed the whole spectacle as an empty distraction. For them, the suffering of poor black communities had been cynically appropriated by a pop star whose real agenda was to increase her already immense fortune. Contrary to claims made on social media, this view wasn't just held by white critics harbouring hidden racist agendas (though there were plenty of those). One clearly upset African American blogger, Isayaah Parker, declared: 'I am insulted by what Beyoncé is doing. Hurricane Katrina happened some ten years ago and here you are, a decade later having the nerve to brush over that shit for profit in the "Formation" video. You made this video so you can make millions of dollars'. What seemed to wrangle Parker most was the image of Beyoncé expressing her solidarity with poor black communities while wearing a $3,000 Gucci outfit. My friend, the always politically astute black British singer

Gina Foster, shared Parker's view. She Facebook-posted a quote from Bobby Seale, co-founder of the Black Panther Party: 'Working class people of all colours must unite against the exploitative, oppressive ruling class. Let me emphasise again – we believe our fight is a class struggle, not a race struggle.' Foster added her own conclusion, 'The revolution should not be monetised!'

Others fist-pumped the air along with the dancers in celebration. 'You See . . . ! We always loved Bey and tonight she has proved that she is ours – our friend, our spokesperson, our source of courage and pride. The revolution WILL be televised, and at prime time.' *The Daily Show*'s Jessica Williams gushed: 'There is so much in this video about black female empowerment. But it's not just about self-love. I mean, she called out police brutality and the constant fear that black people have of the police . . . So what is wrong with Beyoncé everyone? Were you not entertained!?' In line with the pop-loving cultural studies types we looked at earlier, fans like Williams saw this as a moment in popular culture that mattered. Beyoncé had delivered a bold, brave and beautifully executed blow against racism and the powers that be.

So let's use some of what we've discussed to unravel this. Let's start with the least important question: her motives. Yes – it's possible that Beyoncé's embrace of politics was a tactical manoeuvre intended to attract media attention and secure chart positions. It's also possible that she's sincere – or a bit of both. I don't know and won't waste time speculating. What we do know is her suggested political solution to the problems faced. The last line of 'Formation' states: 'Always stay gracious, the best revenge is your paper.' In the video, Beyoncé, who is immaculately styled in Gucci/Channel/Zimmerman/Fendi/Alessandra Rich/Fallon etc., clarifies what 'paper' means by rubbing her thumb and fingers together in the universal sign for cash. 'Beat the bastards by getting rich' is a convenient conclusion for one of the world's highest-earning artists. By her logic, the wealthier she, as an African American woman, becomes, the more she is part of the solution. Other African American artists took a different approach, arguing that the US needs less inequality brought about by a redistribution of wealth. For hip-hop artist Killer Mike, hope was not found on the bottom line of his own bank balance, but the bottom up movement for Senator Bernie Sanders' presidential campaign, which was dramatically gaining ground at the same time Beyoncé dropped 'Formation'. When introducing Sanders at a rally in Atlanta, Georgia, Mike said:

> I am here as a proponent of a political revolution that says healthcare is a right of every citizen. I'm here because working-class and poor people deserve a chance at economic freedom, and yes, if you work 40 hours a week you should NOT be in poverty . . . I truly

believe that senator Bernie Sanders is the right man to lead this country . . . because he, unlike any other candidate, said [he wants to] end this illegal war on drugs that disproportionately targets minorities and poor . . . He says education should be free for every citizen of this country . . . .

Beyoncé and Mike may disagree about the solutions, but both took a decision in 2016 to get political. And not just the 'I Have A Dream, now realised in Obama' stuff that we've seen from Beyoncé before. For all the haute couture, the 'Formation' video did make explicit references to the on-going state terrorism being meted out by police departments in poor neighbourhoods across the US. That was ground-breaking. The most important questions concern not Beyoncé's personal motives or suggested solutions but her timing . . . Racism, police brutality and poverty have been scourges on African American communities her whole life. The Black Panthers were at their zenith nearly 50 years ago and Hurricane Katrina took place more than a decade ago. So what changed for Beyoncé in 2016? As we have seen throughout this book, ideas do not drop into artists' heads from the heavens. All art emerges from a particular time, place and set of social relations.

To understand Beyoncé's decision to get political, we must look beyond her. Killer Mike's story suggests the direction we need to look in. He is a long-term activist and has become a spokesperson for a new and unprecedented movement for racial, social and economic justice in the US. The movement represents a coming together of Occupy activists; workers inspired by the strikes of Chicago and Seattle teachers, among many others; and the Black Lives Matter campaign. The latter started as a hashtag – #blacklivesmatter – on social media following the acquittal of the killer of the (completely innocent and unarmed) African American teenager, Trayvon Martin. It gained national recognition after mobilising street protests following the death at the hands of the police of Michael Brown in Ferguson and Eric Garner in New York City in 2016.

By early 2016, Black Lives Matter had gone nationwide. Key spokespeople from the movement endorsed Sanders, helping to propel the self-described socialist into pole position in some states, in the race to become the Democratic Party's presidential candidate. It also created a climate in which Beyoncé's team thought it expedient (for one reason or another) to get political. The key factor was the growing number of ordinary Americans who were no longer willing to have their needs ignored and communities terrorised. In very different ways, Bernie Sanders and Beyoncé both reflected and helped to articulate those feelings. It was the courage and determination not of pop stars, but of everyday people, that started to reshape the cultural and political landscape.

The Black Lives Matter campaign and broader movement for change continues to grow. In the coming period, with the election of the openly racist and misogynistic Donald Trump as US President, it is likely to be more critical than ever. It faces many challenges. One is the need to find effective political organisation and representation. Hillary Clinton eventually outflanked Sanders to become the Democratic Party's presidential nominee in 2016. Significant numbers of voters, fed up with the status quo, decided not to turn out for the long-term member of the Washington political elite, enabling Trump to take the presidency. Sanders, the left-winger who so enthused young people across the nation, is isolated in the Senate, despite the popularity of his ideas. The Democrat's entrenched pro-big business agenda and affiliations make the party unfit as a vehicle for meaningful change.

Narrow interpretations of identity politics, set in opposition to class consciousness, could also hold the movement back. Such ideas can divide working-class people of different ethnicities and nationalities who could unite around shared concerns.

It is perhaps unlikely that multi-millionaires like Beyoncé will have ongoing relevance to this movement of the streets. But cultural moments like her performance of 'Formation' at the Super Bowl provide opportunities. When one of the world's biggest pop stars gets political in this way, a space is momentarily forced open in the mainstream media for debate. That gives the movement publicity and a chance to grow. Whether the opportunity is seized depends on the degree to which activists can persuade more people to join the cause and get organised.

CHAPTER EIGHT

Their Music

Beyoncé's performance at the Super Bowl provides yet another example of the numerous ways in which the agenda of media moguls and big business can be challenged. Regardless of her personal motives or political limitations, she joins a long tradition of musicians who have used the platform granted to them by music to promote progressive ideas. I've often been bewildered by the reviews and opinion pieces that seem to pop up with regularity bemoaning the death of 'protest music'. I must have seen at least a dozen over the last few years. Often it's a classic case of middle-aged white men seeing the world through the ever-narrowing lens of their own conservative taste. In reality, plenty of musicians continue to consciously grapple with political issues in different ways – they just might not sound like the Clash. But if some pundits need to broaden their outlook, we must remember to keep ours broad too. We should resist the urge to cherry-pick the best examples of musicians getting political while ignoring the majority of the output of the culture industries. Though it has to appeal to a

mass audience, mainstream culture is still disproportionately shaped by its paymasters – with immense wealth
comes considerable influence. It will tend to reflect their
ideas and values. So, what is the ruling class's preferred
soundtrack to the twenty-first century? How are they
using music to defend and extend their privilege and
power now? What new ways have they devised to vet
those occasionally unruly and opinionated stars?

False Idols

The New Zealand band True Bliss are worthy of a
footnote in the history of contemporary culture, not
because of their music, but the way in which they found
fame. In 1999, they were the first winners of a televised
talent show screened in New Zealand called *Popstars*.
The band was soon forgotten, but the concept of the
show was picked up in the UK by London Weekend
Television, and after one season re-branded as *Pop Idol* by
music moguls Simon Cowell and Simon Fuller. In 2002,
the final of *Pop Idol* (UK) attracted 15 million viewers
and some 8.7 million phone votes (there was no limit on
the number of votes an individual viewer could cast).

Similar TV talent shows went on to dominate not only
viewer ratings but also music charts around the world. A
quick look at the format they share is revealing. First and
foremost, music is presented as a competition. Artists
are either jubilant winners or distraught losers. Their

fate is nominally in the hands of a voting public – like countries with parliamentary elections, there's a veneer of democracy. But the parameters of the democratic process (who gets selected to take part) are set by an unelected panel of 'experts', who also have disproportionate influence over how each act is perceived by viewers. Whoever wins, the same multinational companies profit, since a condition for entering the competition is the signing of an exclusive contract with those companies. So, there's a fetishisation of competition, a pseudo-democracy, and fixed economic outcomes that profit the already rich and powerful. This is music mirroring much of what's worst in capitalist society as a whole.

Advertising and Sponsorship

One of the oldest uses of music by the ruling class remains one of the most important, both for them and for musicians. We musicians have long been paid to bring a persuasive emotional quality to rulers' claims. These days, those claims often surround the products corporations are selling. With the relative decline in revenue from record sales in the twenty-first century, the writing or licensing of music for adverts or films – synchronisation with picture, or 'syncs' – is increasingly important for musicians, publishers, managers, music supervisors and various other industry slickers without portfolio. This is music as 'emotion lotion' – as legendary music producer Quincy Jones once put it – liberally applied to images.

It's important to acknowledge that syncs offer huge rewards for musicians – not only from the fees, but also from exposure. Numerous fantastic pieces of music reached a mass audience through TV or film soundtracks. For example, many of us first heard the music of György Ligeti and Richard Strauss at a screening of *2001 Space Odyssey*; Bartók, in *The Shining* and Wagner, in *Apocalypse Now*. Compositions for the big-screen continue to produce some of the most interesting and exciting new music. Of course, the political impact of TV and film music depends on the political agenda of the programme or film. Most big budget productions reflect and reinforce ideas that sit comfortably with corporate funders and distributors. But some make very important progressive statements. All are the result of political contestation between different parties with different agendas and ideas.

There's something more inherently troubling about corporate advertising. It represents the deployment of music in a fundamentally dishonest and cynical way. Any art that moves us, does so because it evokes our emotions – we *feel* it. For this to happen, artists must honestly explore and articulate their feelings about a situation or subject. It could be heartbreak, sexual desire, frustration with work, Paris in the Spring, love, war, rebellion, death, or any number of things. Artists may draw on their experiences directly or imagine what these things feel like. But in advertising, the music is rarely inspired by an experience of the product being sold. Musicians don't gaze at a box of washing powder, evaluate the effectiveness of its detergents and breathe in its aromas, before sketching out ideas. Instead, in step with all the other advertising creatives, we aim for the list of desirable emotional states described on the mood board – 'comfort', 'vitality', 'dependability' or whatever – and do our part to persuade the consumer that those are the qualities on offer in the product whether or not they really are.

If the client can afford it, they will often choose a well-known track for their campaign, in the hope the target audience's associations with it transfer to the product. This is the same fundamental deceit executed in full view. We all know José Gonzalez's 'Heartbeats' wasn't inspired by a Sony TV. But Sony want us to believe that the song, the stunning image of thousands of colourful balls bouncing in slow motion through the streets of San Francisco and their product all somehow belong together. As we pause in reverie at the beauty of the music and images, the advertiser slips their client's logo into our open hearts. We see their sleight of hand, but feel seduced by the whole experience anyway. This is music as honey-trap – enticing us with its pleasures and eliciting misplaced affections.

Whether or not corporations directly commission or license music for adverts, they can still position their brands in its reflected 'cool' by sponsoring music events. To understand the significance of this strategy, we must remember why music and music events are considered 'cool'. I suggested earlier that music helps us to feel connected. It abates our sense of alienation and gives us an exhilarating taste of unity. Put simply, it feels amazing to share great music. No wonder the corporations want to associate their brands with that feeling. Visible corporate sponsorship is now an integral part of most big music events. It's so commonplace it's easy to forget what a juxtaposition this would appear to festival goers in previous decades. After all, the roots of contemporary popular music festivals are closely linked to the hippie movement and a desire to create an alternative space where radical ideas, at least implicitly critical of corporate capitalism, could be explored. Certainly there was a naivety about the endeavour and opportunists would have been there from the start. But it's only in the last two decades that we've seen festivals and areas within festivals named after corporate brands rather than places and music genres. The same is true of carnival – a tradition born of political resistance and long repressed by colonial authorities. Now multinational companies – some of whom make huge profits by extracting natural resources from once colonised countries – attempt to curry favour by sponsoring stages or steel bands. A traditional part of carnival is the masked procession, or 'mas' (masquerade). Sponsorship of carnival, it seems, has become a key corporate PR tactic – an opportunity to create, if you will, masks of corporate benevolence.

Music plays a similar role in commercial radio and music websites. The styles may be very different on Classic FM, Kiss, Heart or the NME, but the function is the same: music delivers its audience to the advertisers.

Music and the Muck of Ages

'The muck of ages' is how Karl Marx once described backwards ideas and old prejudices. A good deal of the music industry continues to be pretty mucky. The story of white imitators being championed over black innovators is as old as the record business. It continues to be a problem. When black artists do appear in the mainstream they are all too often presented in ways that conform to racist stereotypes – black men as gangsters or pimps preoccupied with sex and money. Women – especially black women – continue to be objectified in quite an extreme way, reduced to their 'twerking' buttocks in near pornographic videos or even, in the case of the video for the huge Pharrell Williams and Robin Thicke 2014 hit 'Blurred Lines', explicitly likened to animals.

While artists are rightly reprimanded for such mucky choices, the key architects too often slip away unchallenged. As Pharrell Williams is grilled by interviewers and Sinead O'Connor and Miley Cyrus trade brutal public salvos about appropriate behaviour, music moguls quaff their Dom Pérignon and quietly get richer in blissful seclusion. These are the people who encourage and profit from such controversy. This is where the muck starts and the buck stops. Most aren't conscious-class warriors seeking to divide and rule by promoting racism and sexism. They're looking for easy money. Their prejudice is probably more lazy default than conspiracy, but still it pollutes our sense of ourselves and each other. It gives people – in particular the young – a very narrow view of what it means to be black, masculine, feminine, sexy, or cool. It can also be hugely detrimental to music. To get the support of major labels, women and black musicians all too often have to remodel themselves according to the blinkered vision of wealthy, middle-aged, mostly white men. UK pop/grime artist Lady Leshurr declined a deal with Atlantic Records in the USA after she was told 'Nicki Minaj is your competition and we'll blow her out of the water'. Leshurr reflected that 'It pushes the gaps between us – girl rappers are afraid to work together because we get fixed in these imaginary competitions. The industry just doesn't know what to do with women.'[1] It doesn't help that only 32 per cent of record company employees are female, with the figure dropping in more senior positions.[2] Women accounted for less than 10 per cent of Billboard's 2016 Power 100 list, and black women less than 2 per cent. When female rapper and broadcaster A. Dot was taken on as an A&R consultant at Parlophone in the UK, she found she was the only female on her team and the only black person on the whole floor.[3]

The 'muck of ages' also endures in more subtle ways, just beyond the mainstream. Take, for example, the marketing of 'world music'. Many fans of the various genres that fall under that dubious umbrella title consider themselves to be relatively enlightened. After all, they've often made more of an effort than most to respectfully explore and understand the cultures of others. But even within this cosmopolitan scene, the imprint of backward ideas persists, as I was reminded when asked to review Rough Trade's 2CD compilation of contemporary African music, *Africa 13*. It was undoubtedly one of the better curated and presented compilations released that year. But the idea that a continent as geographically huge and culturally diverse as Africa could be meaningfully represented on two CDs is problematic. What's more, the compilation seemed to reflect a certain nostalgia from its compilers which gave a misleading impression of Africa in 2013. With some excellent exceptions, it favoured the music of older generations over the sounds you would most likely have heard on the streets of the continent's capitals. The hugely popular new Ghanaian genres of hip-life and azonto were absent, but the highlife veteran Ebo Taylor was included. Afrobeat from the 1970s was represented but not contemporary Nigerian afrobeats (that final 's' signifies a whole new US rhythm and bass inspired genre that swept the country in the first decade of the twenty-first century). There's nothing inherently wrong with this – highlife and afrobeat should be celebrated and brought to a wider audience. But such nostalgia crops up a lot in 'world music' marketing. I suspect it reflects an unwitting desire by some fans to exaggerate difference. For them, 'world music' provides an escape to an imaginary place of authenticity and exoticism – the more 'naïve', or 'primitive' it sounds, the better. Fed up with the rat-race? Take a trip to a pre-capitalist idyll where the sounds of smiling natives will sooth away the stresses of modernity . . . Even in this, a scene associated with respectful cultural curiosity, people's perceptions and expectations are still distorted by quasi-colonial values. Even here, we find evidence of alienation, racism and inequality.

Another undeniable whiff of the muck of ages is found in the story of electronic music. Found at the opposite end of the marketing spectrum to 'world music', this is the genre most associated with new technology. It has benefited from a relatively high number of women innovators. Before it was even accepted as music by the mainstream, Daphne Oram and Delia Derbyshire of the BBC Radiophonic Workshop were helping to popularise its appeal. Derbyshire famously created the theme tune and much of the incidental music for the hugely popular British TV show *Doctor Who*. Massive weekly TV audiences were thrilled by her radical new sounds, paving the way for other electronic music innovators. Among the most important were numerous other women including Wendy Carlos, Doris Norton, Suzanne Ciani, Éliane Radigue, Clara Rockmore, Pauline Oliveros, Cynthia Webster and Laurie Anderson. Their contribution is too often overlooked. It also makes the available statistics about gender and electronic music all the more disappointing. Female electronic music initiative Female:Pressure gathered data to establish the gender percentages of artists featured on label releases, festival line-ups and top 100 sales charts. They found 'a 10% proportion of female artists can be considered above average' with most findings putting female representation at between 5 and 8 per cent. If the figures are accurate, then electronic music is even worse than the average across the industry. In 2016, the Performing Right Society (PRS) – a UK based collection agency for composers and songwriters – reported that 16 per cent of their members were female. Despite their crucial role in the history of electronic music, women are still more likely to be found scantily clad on the cover design than in the credits for the writing or production.

The stench also emits from classical music. Astoundingly, the Berlin Philharmonic didn't appoint its first female musician until 1982 and the Vienna Philharmonic remained closed to women until 1997. Things have improved significantly in the intervening years, but chief conductor of the Oslo Philharmonic, Vasily Petrenko, still thought it acceptable in 2014 to claim that orchestras respond better to male conductors. He asserted that men 'often have less sexual energy and can focus more on the music', adding 'a sweet girl on the podium can make one's thoughts drift towards something else'. When she was told about his remarks, acclaimed American conductor Marin Alsop said: 'Petrenko's comments are symptomatic of the covert acceptance of sexism in the musical world.'

Often, when journalists and other commentators challenge one form of prejudice, they reinforce another. They fight muck with muck. For example, many only seem able to find sexism or homophobia in hip-hop, grime or reggae, arguably revealing their own racism. Likewise, they disproportionately scrutinise the choices of female performers. This is still sexist even if their conclusion is that the artist plays too much to the male gaze. There's a lot of hypocrisy in all the muck slinging.

Finally, there is the question of class. Whatever your gender or ethnicity, you are more likely to have success if you come from money. The more glamorous jobs in this industry, as in every other, tend to be grabbed by the rich kids. In 2016, *The Economist* reported that pop stars are more than twice as likely than average to have received a private education.[4] I'd wager that in music industry boardrooms, the situation is even more skewed. The conclusion that being born to wealth helps you climb the corporate ladder is so obvious that few would challenge it. As the Labour MP and former shadow culture minister Chris Bryant observed: 'The truth is that people who subsidise the arts most are artists themselves. That of course makes it much more difficult if you come from a background where you can't afford to do that.' (Rich, white, male) pop star James Blunt disagreed. His rather nasty right-wing reply to Bryant did at least make an attempt at wit:

Dear Chris Bryant MP,

You classist gimp . . . What you teach is the politics of jealousy. Rather than celebrating success and figuring out how we can all exploit it further as the Americans do, you instead talk about how we can hobble that success and 'level the playing field'. Perhaps what you've failed to realise is that the only head-start my school gave me in the music business, where the VAST majority of people are NOT from boarding school, is to tell me that I should aim high. Perhaps it protected me from your kind of narrow-minded, self-defeating, lead-us-to-a-dead-end, remove-the-'G'-from-'GB' thinking, which is to look at others' success and say, 'it's not fair.'

Up yours,
James Cucking Funt.[5]

To which Bryant replied:

Dear James

... I'm delighted you've done well for yourself. But it is really tough forging a career in the arts if you can't afford the enormous fees for drama school, if you don't know anybody who can give you a leg up, if your parents can't subsidise you for a few years whilst you make your name and if you can't afford to take on an unpaid internship ...

We need more diversity at every level in the arts – in education, in training, on-screen, on stage and backstage – and we need to break down all the barriers to taking part so that every talent gets a chance.

Yours bluntly,
Chris.[6]

Even now, as we approach the end of the second decade of the twenty-first century, the music industry is still influenced by old-school ties with lazy stereotyping its default setting. The ruling ideas of our times remain those of the ruling class. In ways both obvious and subtle, the muck of ages continues to pollute our culture and with it our communities and minds.

Secret Spin Masters and Cultural Colonisation

Earlier we touched on the CIA's involvement in a covert cultural cold war. I asked Francis Stonor Saunders, author of an excellent book on the subject, *Who Paid the Piper?*, whether she thought similar operations continue today. She pointed out that if they were conducted properly, we simply wouldn't know about them, but then related a revealing conversation she had with former British Prime Minister Gordon Brown. Apparently, he was a fan of the book but had somehow missed the author's view, implicit throughout, that such clandestine meddling in culture was a bad thing. After lavishing praise on the work, he remarked that the British government should look into using the same tactics to combat 'extremism' today. I suspect the CIA has beaten him to it. In his book *Living the Hiplife*, Jesse Weaver Shipley quotes an unnamed US cultural attaché to Accra. The source acknowledged that US government agencies actively promote American hip-hop in Africa, because they believe it improves the country's image, and acts as an alternative pole of attraction to radical Islam.[7] That's quite something. If true, then we have a situation where music created by the descendants of slaves is now a tool for promoting the image of the US in the countries their ancestors were placed in chains. It's a dizzying act of political spin. In truth it's a contradiction American rulers would probably have preferred to avoid – it's doubtful that hip-hop was then Secretary of State Hillary Clinton's first choice for musical diplomacy. But much as soul music won West African hearts and minds in the 1970s, so hip-hop seems to be the American music that resonates most now.

From the perspective of the powerful, when voices from marginalised communities start to resonate globally, they must be silenced or co-opted.

The US Information Agency was disbanded in 1999, but Voice of America radio continues to broadcast in five English language versions and 41 other languages. When I visited Ghana recently, it was VOA that my host tuned into as we sat in Accra's rush hour traffic. When I asked her why she'd chosen that station, she shrugged and said it played the best music. Critics continue to make the accusation that it's a propaganda tool, pointing out that the Secretary of State continues to sit on its board of governors.

Even without covert operations, the economic clout of America's culture industry allows it to grab the attention of a global audience. Those who control culture in the US disproportionately influence it everywhere else. The result is not only the ubiquity of baseball caps, hip-hop and linguistic Americanisms, but also a generalised sense that America is 'cool'. If a president is seen hanging out with Jay Z and Beyoncé, young people around the world may be better disposed towards that president. The impact is impossible to quantify, but just as African leaders Nyerere and Nkrumah feared in the 1960s, the export of American culture continues to smooth the way for other interventions.

CHAPTER NINE

My Turn

With a greater awareness of what's going on comes a responsibility to act. I was in a successful band with a growing media presence: that gave me a platform and some leverage. I felt it was worth trying to use those things to promote progressive ideas and provoke debate. My attempts to do so started modestly. When I first appeared on the music TV show *Later With Jools Holland* I wore a T-shirt in solidarity with Liverpool dockers who were on strike at the time. I had 'Love Music Hate Racism' logos displayed on the big screens during a Faithless UK arena tour in the run up to an election being contested by the racist British National Party. Between tours, I made political music of my own with my band Slovo and persuaded Maxi Jazz from Faithless to join me for a performance in Trafalgar Square for the Stop The War Coalition. I also wrote opinion pieces, gave interviews and generally got active with radical left-wing and anti-war movements. For a while, I was a proud member of the Socialist Workers Party. When they first asked me to join, I told them that artists should remain politically independent. They soon persuaded me this was pretentious nonsense. Though I'm no longer a member, I still think they're right about that. It's good to be a joiner. I'm sure I bored some of my bandmates silly with my barstool/tour-bus rants. But on the whole they respected and approved of my actions. I was happy with my work and my activism. In fact, I felt incredibly lucky and fulfilled. I wasn't looking for another political cause – but one found me. Little did I know I was beginning a journey that would eventually lead to my receiving death threats, being condemned on Fox News as 'evil' and branded a troublemaker by the bosses of the band I'd been proud to be associated with for nearly two decades.

The Question of Cultural Boycott

It all started in 1999, when Faithless first visited Israel. We'd played at a rave on a beach somewhere south of Tel Aviv and the after-show had become a haze of mojitos, merriment and late night swimming in the Mediterranean. The following morning, with a sore head and a mouth dryer than the Negev desert, I contemplated how to spend my day off. Most of the band drifted slowly back to the beach, but I made different plans. I'd heard a bit about the political situation in the region and wanted to see for myself what life was like for Palestinians.

I stepped out into the rising heat to begin the short but complicated journey from Tel Aviv to Gaza. Playwright David Hare once likened the same trip to hopping from California to Bangladesh. Certainly the poverty I witnessed when I arrived in Gaza shocked me. Just off the main Al Nassar Street, scrawny teenagers guided donkeys along sand-covered lanes while craftsmen fixed shoes on ancient-looking machinery. In the rubble of one of Gaza's refugee camps, groups of men, prevented from travelling to work in Israel, crowded around games of backgammon, while ragged-looking children kicked oranges around or played tag in the dirt. It was obvious Gaza got few visitors – I was eyed with friendly curiosity. 'Welcome to Gaza' was shouted from passing cars and everywhere I went seats were pulled up for me and small cups of sweet mint tea were offered. There seemed to be a sense of approval and appreciation that I had bothered to visit. When my nationality was established I was sternly lectured about something called the Balfour Agreement. Apparently it implicated Britain in this whole mess. In a shabby park with a large new monument to martyred soldiers, a young woman wearing a hijab approached me, keen to practise her English. She explained that the Israelis had turned Gaza into a prison – a prison for those whose only crime was being Palestinian.

In 2005, Faithless returned to play a music festival in Haifa. By this time I had made several trips to Palestine – mostly to the West Bank where I had worked with members of a hip-hop crew called the Ramallah Underground. Their rapper, Boikutt, featured on my second Slovo album. Since Ramallah was so close, I invited Boikutt to the Faithless show. He thanked me, but explained that the checkpoints, 'separation' wall and Israeli-only roads that dissect the West Bank would make the short journey impossible. He added that as a supporter of the cultural boycott of Israel, he would rather we weren't performing there at all. At that time I knew of no Western bands or artists who supported the boycott. Many had been persuaded that Israel was largely the innocent victim of regional politics rather than the perpetrator of state terrorism and apartheid. After all, that was the view peddled by most of the British mainstream media who faithfully echoed the attitudes of the UK and US governments. Since the 1950s, I later learned, both have seen it as in their strategic interests to give political cover to Israel – as well as economic and military support. Soon after that conversation with Boikutt, public attitudes started to change, due mainly to the brutal actions of the Israeli state.

First came Israel's massive assault on Lebanon in 2006 – allegedly in retaliation for the abduction of two Israeli soldiers by Hezbollah. The conflict cost at least 1,200 lives – mainly Lebanese citizens – and ended in defeat for the Israeli army. Next was 'Operation Cast Lead' – Israel's shocking bombardment of Gaza between December 2008 and January 2009, in which 1,385 Palestinians were killed, 318 of them children.[1] Just one year later, an international flotilla of boats attempting to bring aid to besieged Gaza was attacked in international waters by the Israeli Army. A UN report concluded that Israeli soldiers opened fire with live rounds before illegally boarding a ship. Nine activists died, six of them – one American and five Turkish citizens – in execution-style killings. There were no Israeli fatalities. Anger at each of these events erupted in demonstrations and student occupations across the world.

The siege of Gaza affected me most deeply. A UN fact-finding mission described it as 'a deliberately disproportionate attack designed to punish, humiliate and terrorise a civilian population, radically diminish its local economic capacity both to work and to provide for itself, and to force upon it an ever increasing sense of dependency and vulnerability'.[2] I learned more about 'Operation Cast Lead' following an offer from my friend Jen Marlowe – a filmmaker, writer and activist from the US. She asked me to compose music for *One Family in Gaza*, her short film telling the story of the Awajah family – one among thousands subjected to the attack. In it, Waffa Awajah describes how her son Ibrahim – an unarmed nine-year-old boy – was executed by an Israeli soldier at point-blank range in front of his family. When Waffa pleaded for the lives of the other children, the soldier laughed. Unable to retrieve Ibrahim's body for fear of also being killed, the family hid through the night.

Waffa watched while Israeli soldiers used her son's body for target practise.[3]

Mounting public awareness of Israel's crimes meant that more ordinary people were moved to speak up – among them musicians, writers and artists. Palestinian civil society was calling for boycott, divestment and sanctions (BDS) to be imposed on Israel. The potential to make that a reality was growing.

In 2010, Faithless were once again invited to perform in Israel. Maxi Jazz first raised the question of boycott at a dinner attended by all but one of the band. After some discussion everyone at the dinner agreed we should boycott and that Maxi would write a statement explaining why to the fans:

'All Races All Colours All Creeds Got The Same Needs.'

Hi, this is Maxi Jazz and these are just some of the lyrics I perform every night with my friends known as Faithless. And this short note is for all fans and family of the band in Israel. It's fair to say that for 14 years we've been promoting goodwill, trust and harmony all around the world in our own small (but very loud!) way. Ok. We've been asked to do some shows this summer in your country and, with the heaviest of hearts, I have regretfully declined the invitation. While human beings are being wilfully denied not just their rights but their NEEDS for their children and grandparents and themselves, I feel deeply that I should not be sending even tacit signals that this is either 'normal' or 'ok'. It's neither and I cannot support it. It grieves me that it has come to this and I pray everyday for human beings to begin caring for each other, firm in the wisdom that we are all we have.

We Come 1. maxi[4]

Around this time, several other artists joined the boycott, including Elvis Costello, the Pixies, Massive Attack, Gil Scott-Heron, Santana, Roger Waters, Devendra Banhart, Tindersticks, Pete Seeger, Cassandra Wilson and Cat Power. Its growth worried both the Israeli government and their international supporters. In early 2012, a group of 30 leading music executives, agents and lawyers were invited to the law offices of Ziffren Brittenham in Los Angeles by an organisation called Creative Community for Peace. This well-funded group was set up by former Chairman and CEO of Universal Music Publishing Group, David Renzer, and worldwide head of music for EA video games, Steve Schnur. Its sole objective was to prevent artists joining the boycott.[5] When singer Macy Gray expressed serious doubts about performing in Israel, Renzer and Schnur stepped in. They argued that performing in Israel would benefit both Israelis and Palestinians and added that if she went, they would fund the donation of an ambulance to United

Hatzalah – an organisation of Israeli medical volunteers. Macy agreed to go.

Some critics of the boycott ask why Israel is singled out when so many states behave badly. It's worth pointing out that it's a perverse logic that says we can't criticise one state just because another is even worse. The people who pose the question are often implicitly making the charge of anti-Semitism. They claim that to criticise Israel is to be anti-Jewish. This idea conflates Zionism – the political movement that founded the Jewish state – with Judaism. Zionists have systematically attempted to make such a conflation. I reject it. As the editors of the Independent Jewish Voices book *A Time to Speak Out* state:

> It is because successive Israeli governments claim to represent Jews in general, a claim that is as groundless as it is injurious, that it is vital to speak out. Moreover in the United Kingdom those who claim to speak for British Jews collectively (or allow that impression to go unchallenged) tend to reflect only one position on Israel's conflicts: that of the Israeli government. In reality, however, there is a broad spectrum of opinion among Jews in Britain – just as there is among any other Jewish population in the world – on Israel and on Zionism. Many Jews refuse to view these subjects through a narrow ethnocentric lens. They base their opinions instead upon universal principles of justice

and human rights. And they refuse to accept that Israel alone offers a viable identity for Jews.[6]

Labelling all critics of Israel anti-Semitic is like labelling all opponents of apartheid in South Africa anti-white. In fact, the struggle against anti-Semitism is undermined by Zionists who claim to represent all Jews and who denounce all opposition to Israeli government policy as anti-Semitic. This is a bullying tactic used to suppress opposition. As David Clark, former adviser to the Labour government in Britain in the 1990s, puts it:

When I hear people argue that Israel is unfairly singled out, I wish I could persuade myself that what they mean is: 'If only people cared as much about the people of Tibet/Darfur/Zimbabwe as they do for the Palestinians'. But ... I suspect that what they often mean is: 'If only people cared as little for the Palestinians as they do for the people of Tibet/Darfur/Zimbabwe'.[7]

Besides, an absence of calls for cultural boycott elsewhere is not necessarily evidence of Israel being singled out for criticism. Boycott is not a universal principle that can be applied in every situation – it is a political tactic. In most situations it would be the wrong one. Many artists oppose the brutal regimes in Saudi Arabia and Bahrain for example, but it's a bit meaningless to call for a boycott if you've never been asked to play there in the first place. Israel by contrast, is somewhere a cultural boycott can have a real impact. The country is carefully branded by its government as the regional centre for all things cool, sexy and Western. Tel Aviv is promoted as a hedonistic, open-minded party city – an image made credible by frequent visits by some of the world's best known bands and DJs. This manufactured image matters to Israel. The implicit message is that the country is liberal and progressive. Music fans can dance, drink and party long into the night, blissfully distracted from the suffering endured by Palestinians. In effect, music helps to drown out the cries of the oppressed in a society wilfully in denial of its role as oppressor. I decided to support the cultural boycott because I see it as a refusal to be complicit in this crime. It is a nonviolent and effective way to highlight the reality of what's going on and to apply pressure for change. Perhaps most importantly, boycott is what Palestinian civil society – those on the sharp end of oppression – has asked of us.

Opponents of the cultural boycott sometimes argue that it punishes the wrong people – that music fans are among those most likely to oppose their government's policies. But gigs don't take place in a political or economic vacuum. No matter how enlightened a particular artist's fans may be, or how progressive the band's message, performing in Israel can all too easily be interpreted by the wider world as an endorsement of an apartheid state. The Israeli government knows this. It has

long recognised the political power of culture. As Brian
Eno explained when he decided not to allow his music to
be used by the Israeli dance company Batsheva:

> To my understanding, the Israeli Embassy (and
> therefore the Israeli government) will be sponsoring
> the upcoming performances, and, given that I've
> been supporting the BDS campaign for several years
> now, this is an unacceptable prospect for me. It's
> often said by opponents of BDS that art shouldn't be
> used as a political weapon. However, since the Israeli
> government has made it quite clear that it uses art in
> exactly that way – to promote 'Brand Israel' and to
> draw attention away from the occupation of Palestinian
> land – I consider that my decision to deny permission
> is a way of taking this particular weapon out of their
> hands . . . I feel that your government exploits artists
> like you, playing on your natural desire to keep working
> – even if it does mean becoming part of a propaganda
> strategy. Your dance company might not be able to
> formally distance itself from the Israeli government but
> I can and will: I don't want my music to be licensed for
> any event sponsored by the Israeli embassy.

I discussed this with my friend Ohal, an Israeli artist
and another supporter of BDS, and I know that she and
her Israeli BDS colleagues can understand the need
for a boycott. As artists we should be free to choose

to respond to the injustices of governments, yours or mine.[8]

When Faithless joined the boycott, our manager and one leading band member strongly disagreed with the decision. They pressured Maxi to change his mind, believing the rest of us would follow. Other artists I've spoken to describe similar pressures from managers or others in the industry. Many arrive at the rather pointless compromise of refusing invitations to perform in Israel, while never publicly stating why.

There's also pressure from opponents outside the music industry, as I discovered when I recorded a radio advert for South African Artists Against Apartheid while touring there with Faithless. In the advert I said: 'Hi, I'm Dave Randall from Faithless. Twenty years ago I would not have played in apartheid South Africa – today I refuse to play in Israel. Be on the right side of history. Don't entertain apartheid. Join the international boycott of Israel. I support southafricanartistsagainstapartheid.com'[9]

When the advert aired on mainstream pop radio station SABC's 5FM, the radio station and our concert promoter received complaints. We were warned to expect protests outside the gig and the promoter brought in a lot of extra security to screen ticket holders, raising suspicions that veiled death threats had also been made. As I waited to go onstage, my guitar technician grinned and slapped me on the back. 'I won't take the bullet for you Dave, but don't worry – I'll clean the blood off your guitars.' We laughed nervously. The threats were idle scaremongering – there wasn't a single protestor and the raucous Cape Town audience emanated nothing but love.

Unfortunately, the same couldn't be said backstage. On hearing about the advert, our manager asked me to explain why I'd created a 'shit-storm'. I said I was sorry if that's what he'd experienced, but added that I felt I'd done the right thing. He took a long drag on his cigarette and much like a weary parent berating an insolent child, told me 'the reason why people here are upset is because they've lived through apartheid and know from first-hand experience how wrong you are about Israel'. In terms of being given an opportunity to explain my position, his rather patronising comment was a gift. Unbeknown to him, I'd accepted a lunch invitation that day from the former leader of the armed wing of the ANC and minister of the ANC government, Ronnie Kasrils. I'd emailed him before leaving the UK asking to interview him for a series of 'Randall Report' tour diary videos I was producing. During that interview he categorically refuted the manager's claim. Kasrils is convinced Israel *is* currently practising a form of apartheid and he fully supports the BDS movement. He added that South African anti-apartheid veteran Archbishop Desmond Tutu and the Congress of South African Trade Unions did too. In the words of Nelson Mandela, 'our freedom is incomplete without the freedom of the Palestinians.'

I told the manager. He pulled again on his cigarette and looked away in what I took to be an acknowledgement that he wouldn't win the political argument.

But as I would learn, there are drawbacks to having smart-arse answers for irate managers. I think, in that moment, I ceased to be a 'likeable leftie who needs to be reined-in', in his mind. Now I was a 'troublemaker who must be purged'. The next day a statement appeared on the Faithless website apologising for 'any offence caused by the views expressed by guitarist Dave Randall' adding that the views 'were not representative of the rest of the band'. It was an odd move since it drew more attention to a matter previously confined to the airwaves of South Africa. And it was based on an odd premise – that *some* band members are not entitled to air their views. Or was it that band members are not entitled to air *certain* views? Or both? Maxi has said in numerous interviews that he is a Buddhist and a lover of motor racing. Management didn't issue a public statement reassuring fans that we're not all *namyo-herengi-kyo*-chanting petrol heads. The difference, of course, is that my views on Israel were considered to be potentially damaging to brand Faithless. In the last few years there had been an increasing number of presumably very lucrative corporate tie-ins – most recently with Coca-Cola, Tesco and Fiat. Management wanted to preserve an 'investor friendly' image and a guitarist banging on about Palestine was not part of the script.

My Campaign Song

Having become aware of the issues facing Palestinians, I decided that another small gesture of solidarity I could offer was a song. Its story is worth telling since it shines a light on some of the key changes and new opportunities that came about in the early twenty-first century.

Billy Bragg often points out that in the 1960s, '70s and '80s, songs were the way young people communicated political messages and ideas. Now, he implies, blogging and social media perform that role. Certainly social media provides activists with powerful new tools, but it's misleading to suggest songs no longer matter. Music will always be needed to describe the world and illuminate contradictions in ways words alone cannot. Just because thoughts and reports can now be immediately shared with millions doesn't change that. What the internet *does* change is the relationship between artists and audiences. It gives us the potential to bypass the old gatekeepers of the music industry and mass media and use alternative networks to reach people. The modest successes achieved by my song would not have happened before the internet.

Writing good songs isn't easy – let alone ones that successfully communicate a political message. I knew I couldn't please everybody. Those who already supported the politics might not like the song and those who admired my work as a musician might not like my politics. Such problems have faced everyone who has attempted to make overtly political music. I decided to give it a go anyway . . . What good is music if it can't occasionally 'comfort the disturbed and disturb the comfortable'?

Any perceived criticism of Israel remains controversial, at least in Europe and North America, for the reasons outlined previously. The political purpose of my song was to try to shift solidarity with Palestinians towards the mainstream. There's plenty of excellent moody Arabic hip-hop that talks about Palestine; I wanted to write something that would reach a different audience – people new to the issue. The song needed to be upbeat, accessible, defiant – even a bit 'cheesy'. The music needed to bring a reassuring feeling of the familiar to lyrics that some would find provocative. It also needed to represent the breadth, inclusiveness and internationalism of the solidarity movement, with contributors from different countries, cultures and backgrounds. This internationalism should also be reflected in the artist name.

Centrally important was that Palestinians supported the song and agreed with its objectives. Soon after I had the idea, I visited the West Bank and spoke at length with activists, including Omar Barghouti and Jamal Juma, from respectively the Boycott National Committee and the Stop The Wall campaign. They encouraged me and recorded messages of support. The result was the song 'Freedom for Palestine', released in July 2011 under the name OneWorld. It featured most of the members of Faithless, including Maxi Jazz, my old friend Jamie Catto

from 1 Giant Leap, the British/Iraqi oud player Attab
Haddad, members of the London Community Gospel
Choir and, from South Africa, the Durban Gospel Choir,
who I recorded and filmed on an exhilarating day off
during the 2011 Faithless tour in South Africa. Compared
to the star-studded 1980s anti-apartheid anthem 'Sun
City', it was a modest line-up. But it was enough to get
the message across. Besides, the solidarity movement
for Palestine was at a different stage to that reached by
the movement against apartheid in South Africa in the
eighties. My song would simply be a small step in the right
direction. Any profits would go to projects in Palestine
via the UK-based charity War on Want.

Around the time of the release a senior campaigner at
War on Want, Yasmin Khan, was invited onto Channel
4's satirical panel show *10 O'Clock Live*. Off air, she
took the opportunity to tell one of the presenters, BBC
6 Music's Lauren Laverne, about the song. Laverne
warned Khan that its politics might make it very tricky
to promote at the BBC. She was right – we didn't get
any airplay. In the twentieth century, an independent
single without a marketing budget, airplay, or any other
support from the mainstream media would most likely
have disappeared unnoticed. But by 2011 important new
potential avenues for sharing music had opened up. At
a meeting in central London, activist groups including
War on Want, the Palestine Solidarity Campaign, the
Stop The War Coalition, Friends of Al-Aqsa, Jews for

Justice for Palestinians, Israeli Committee Against House Demolitions UK and the Russell Tribunal agreed to use the song as a centrepiece for a co-ordinated social media campaign. Through those shared networks, we started to reach an audience who spread the word further.

Within days, endorsements flowed in from around the world. The American novelist Alice Walker sent a moving assessment of the song: 'This is what art can do, and what art must do, to help us save what's left of our humanity. "Freedom for Palestine" brought me to my feet to dance with everyone on earth who knows right from wrong and chooses, delightedly, to join the worldwide party of the just.' Pink Floyd's Roger Waters also sent his support: 'I applaud Dave Randall and Maxi Jazz, and all the other musicians who came together to record "Freedom for Palestine". I fully share, and endorse, the sentiments they express in their song, more power to them and to all who stand together in the fight for a free Palestine. We shall overcome.'

The song was also shared in Palestine itself. My old friend Boikutt approvingly reported that all Ramallah was talking about it. Young people in Gaza even created their own video for the song which they uploaded to YouTube.

Next, Billy Bragg and Massive Attack posted endorsements on their Facebook pages triggering huge online discussions. Then Coldplay, one of the biggest bands in the world at the time, shared the following sentence on Facebook: 'Some of our friends are involved in OneWorld's new "Freedom for Palestine" single', and posted a link to the OneWorld website and the video. The post reached several million followers. It was a fleeting and cautious statement, but detonated a massive online argument with thousands of responses both for and against. Coldplay's support was reported in the Israeli newspaper *Haaretz*, Britain's *Guardian,* and countless political blogs around the world. I was delighted – the song was making waves. Next, we received news that Archbishop Desmond Tutu had recorded a video endorsement of the song and that a British Liberal Democrat MP had brought an Early Day Motion to the House of Commons commending it. The motion also called on the government 'to join forces with governments around the world to put pressure on Israel to honour UN resolutions'.

Then came by far the most amusing moment in the campaign. A Fox News item in the US, presented by Glenn Beck, described the song and its creators as evil. Glenn Beck is a right-wing American 'shock-jock'. He spent ten minutes denouncing the song, playing a lengthy section from the video and listing the supporters, including Coldplay, before making an emotional appeal to Hollywood creatives to respond. We couldn't have bought better publicity.

Despite the lack of airplay, the song reached the top ten on the independent chart and number 79 on the mainstream chart in the UK. Nothing spectacular, but chart positions were never the real point. Our mission to raise awareness and start a discussion with a bigger mainstream audience was accomplished.

In the days before the internet, a song released on a tiny independent label under an unknown collective name and excluded or ignored by the mainstream media could never have achieved such success. However, we should be wary of exaggerating how much the internet and social media has changed or 'democratised' the cultural landscape. The discrepancy between the independent and mainstream chart positions tells you something about the continued dominance of the old major labels. Of the top 80 singles that week, 70 belonged to majors. Even the independent chart remains dominated by huge companies such as XL Recordings. Big money still dictates mainstream culture, and life is precarious for the smaller fish of the music industry. Our modest but real achievements were not due to the internet alone. Like so many political songs before mine, 'Freedom for Palestine' still relied on activist networks and organisations. It was the combination of social media and social movements that made success possible.

CHAPTER TEN

Music of the Arab Revolutions

Something similar might be said of the rather more significant sequence of events known briefly as the 'Arab Spring'. Mainstream commentators often overplay the role of social media, insisting that Facebook and Twitter were integral factors – seemingly forgetting that many of the most important revolutions in history took place long before the internet existed. But if the impact of social media is sometimes overstated, what's often ignored altogether is the role played by music. The uprisings were some of the most remarkable events in recent political history, so it's worth discussing their soundtracks. The following musical story traces the same tragic arc as the Arab Spring as a whole. It begins with an optimistic 21-year-old's hip-hop tune and ends with a singer's body washing up on the shores of the Orontes River.

The Arab Spring began in Tunisia in late 2010 with a series of protests and strikes that swept the country resulting in the downfall of the US-backed dictator Zine

El Abidine Ben Ali. Many accounts of the uprising begin on 17 December 2010, with the tragic self-immolation of the fruit-seller Mohamed Bouazizi. There is no doubt the act became a symbolic turning point for the long oppressed masses of Tunisia, but there were other earlier catalysts. One was a tune recorded by Hamada Ben Amor – a young hip-hop artist and fan of US rapper Tupac Shakur. In November 2010, under the name El General, he uploaded the track 'Rais Lebled' (Mr President) to YouTube. The self-produced video began with some vintage news footage of the Tunisian dictator inadvertently reducing a schoolboy to tears in a stage-managed display of his kindness and popularity. The lyrics addressed the president directly: 'You know these words that make your eyes weep, as a father does not want to hurt his children; then this is a message from one of your children who is telling of his suffering; we are living like dogs.'

While the song was a damning assessment of life under Ben Ali, it stopped short of calling for him to go – instead it was a plea for reforms. The dictator is even described as 'a father'. This initially subordinate tone is found time and time again in the histories of revolutions – people begin by telling the powerful how things are in the hope that reforms will follow. When those appeals are ignored or met with repression, radicalisation follows and demands become revolutionary. We can see precisely that pattern here. 'Rais Lebled' was posted on YouTube and Facebook on 7 November 2010 and quickly spread across social networks. Mohamed Bouazizi set himself ablaze on 17 December, leading to an explosion of pro-democracy demonstrations. The protestors' demands were met with tear gas, police batons and brutality. The reaction radicalised the population. On 22 December, El General released a new track called 'Tounes Bledna' (Tunisia is our country):

> Tunisia is our country, with politics or with blood!
> Tunisia is our country and her men will never surrender!
> Tunisia is our country, the whole people hand-in-hand!
> Tunisia is our country and today we must find the solution!

He was no longer trying to 'speak truth to power'. Instead a more militant El General recognised that the only solution lay in the hands of the people. This was a step too far for the regime. El General was considered such a threat that on 6 January 2011, 30 state security officers 'acting on the orders of Ben Ali himself' turned up at his door and threw him into prison. Happily, within one week, mass strikes and the ongoing demonstrations forced Ben Ali to flee the country. El General was released.

'Rais Lebled' wasn't only an important expression of revolutionary currents in Tunisia, it also travelled quickly to Egypt. This is one of the great strengths of music, especially in the internet age. If there isn't a language barrier, protestors on the streets of one country can immediately adopt the songs and chants from the revolution next door – or anywhere else in the world. The chant 'The people demand the removal of the regime' was first heard in Tunisia at the end of 2010. By January 2011, it was reverberating across Egypt.

In Cairo's Tahrir Square, a 23-year-old singer songwriter and part-time student called Ramy Essam listened to the various political chants. Inspired by events in Tunisia, he had joined thousands of other Egyptians who made their way to the square to demand the fall of Egypt's US backed dictator – Hosni Mubarak. Essam felt the chants were becoming stale and repetitive. How much better, he thought, if they were put to music. Equipped with just an acoustic guitar, he set about the task and so became the most important and recognised singer of the Egyptian revolution. The simplicity of his songs and choice of instrument provide a refreshing corrective to the idea that this was a revolution dependent on new technology – the mobile phone and social media. Woody Guthrie and Victor Jara would have felt quite at home onstage with Essam and many of the other singers in the square. Essam's best known song is called 'Irhal' (Leave!).

We are all one hand – have one demand. Down down
Hosni Mubarak!
The people demand the removal of the regime.
Leave! Leave! Leave! Leave!

On 11 February, Mubarak did leave, sending shock-
waves around the world. Faithless were in South Africa
at the time so I joined a lively celebration in solidarity
with Egyptians on the steps of Cape Town's St George's
Cathedral. I recall a clergyman in long dark robes smiling
in the sunshine, and holding aloft a handwritten sign that
simply read 'Democracy Now – from Cape 2 Cairo with
love'. But while Mubarak had left, his generals had not.
Many protestors, including Essam, stayed in the square
to defend and advance the revolution. On 9 March 2011,
the army moved in. Essam was targeted and thrown into a
museum requisitioned by the army as a makeshift prison.
He was badly beaten and tortured. A few days later, after
his release, Essam heroically returned to the square to
continue to sing 'Irhal', but with references to Mubarak
now changed to target the military. At the time of writing,
Egypt remains in the grip of the generals. Essam, who has
been forced to seek exile in Sweden, continues to sing out.

There was another fascinating musical aspect to the
Egyptian revolution. As well as adopting new songs by
Essam and others, protesters also symbolically linked the
struggle against the Western-backed Mubarak with the
anti-imperialist struggle that took place some 90 years

earlier. They did so by reviving the memory of one of Egypt's great musical rebels – Sayed Darwish.

The Palestinian singer Reem Kelani once told me Sayed Darwish was Egypt's equivalent of Woody Guthrie and George Gershwin. Certainly he shared humble origins with those American heroes. Born in 1892 in a working-class district of Alexandria, he balanced music studies with work as a bricklayer to support his family. In 1918, he moved to Cairo to pursue an interest in musical theatre. There he met the playwright and poet Badî' Khayrî, who would become his lifelong friend and collaborator. Together they created a huge body of work chronicling the lives of Egypt's working classes and those at the margins of society. Railway station porters, women workers, minority Nubian communities and even drug addicts became the dignified protagonists of their popular songs and operettas.

Darwish and Khayrî also wrote songs in opposition to religious division and sectarianism – songs calling for unity between Muslims and Christian Copts. Their sincerity is illustrated by the story of the death of Khayrî's father. Darwish went to pay his respects at the local Coptic church, but the funeral procession failed to appear. Confused and concerned, he made his way to Khayrî's house and found the family sitting together reading from the Koran. The fact that Egypt's equivalent to George and Ira Gershwin didn't know each other's religion shows how little dogma and divisions affected them.

Egypt at that time was under British colonial control. Many Egyptians had fought alongside the British during the First World War and expected to be rewarded with independence. British rulers, however, had no intention of handing over such a strategically important land. Egypt, and in particular control of the Suez Canal, were central to their imperialist plans for the region. Ordinary Egyptians became enraged by the situation at the same time as the phonograph – first introduced to Egypt in 1904 – and better distribution of sheet music were extending the reach and influence of composers. Darwish started writing nationalist and pan-Arabist songs. When an uprising took place in 1919, they became its anthems. The story of one such song demonstrates the potential for the social and political meaning of music to change according to circumstance.

Darwish's 'Bilaadi! Bilaadi!' (My homeland! My homeland!) was sung defiantly by Egyptians in 1919. The chorus lyrics were taken from a speech given by Mustafa Kamil Pasha – a fervent Egyptian nationalist and advocate of Egyptian independence:

My homeland, my homeland, my homeland,
You have my love and my heart.

The revolutionaries of 1919 put up a brave fight against the authorities. In a reversal of the events of 2011, when the regime closed down mobile phone networks in an attempt to regain control of the streets, the rebels cut Cairo's phone lines to delay the colonial regime calling London for assistance. Despite their courage and guile, the uprising was eventually defeated. In 1922 Britain did agree to formally recognise Egyptian independence, but it was a cosmetic change rather than a real transition to self-determination and democracy. The leaders of the rebellion were forced into exile. In 1923, aged just 31, Darwish died. Some say he was poisoned, while others believe he suffered a heart attack after a cocaine binge. Either way, the British-backed establishment were delighted to see him gone and did their best to bury his legacy. Darwish was removed from, or ignored by, all establishment accounts of Egyptian music and culture. When, in 1936, Cairo hosted a conference of Arabic music, he didn't get a single mention. But things changed following the overthrow of the monarchy in 1952 and the election of the nationalist Gamal Abdel Nasser in 1956. One of Nasser's first moves as president was to nationalise the Suez Canal, brushing off threats from Britain, France and Israel. This inspired the Arab world. On Egyptian streets 'Bilaadi! Bilaadi!' was heard once again – this time as an unofficial anthem of pan-Arabist pride and unity.

Nasser died of a heart attack in 1970 and was succeeded by Anwar Sadat. The two had been close, but Sadat set Egypt on a very different course to that fought for by Nasser. In the mid-1970s he pushed through unpopular new neoliberal economic policies, which led to rising unemployment and bread shortages. Demonstrations and strikes erupted across the country. Sadat then signed a controversial peace agreement with Israel – seen by most of the Arab world as selling out the long-suffering Palestinians. At this low point for pan-Arabism Sadat adopted 'Bilaadi! Bilaadi!' as Egypt's national anthem. Many people saw this as a cynical betrayal of the radical anthem's message. Therefore, when, in January 2011, Egyptians celebrated the toppling of a Western-backed dictator with proud and joyful renditions of 'Bilaadi! Bilaadi!' they were not only proclaiming their hopes for the nation, but also reclaiming its most iconic song.

As Egyptians celebrated next door, growing numbers of Libyans were taking to the streets in an uprising against the country's leader Colonel Gaddafi. They too had their anthem. 'Sawfa Nabqa Huna' (We Will Remain) was penned by former political prisoner Adel Al Mshiti in 2005 and was shared widely online in early 2011. By March, the mournful ballad was heard on mass demonstrations in major cities across the country. The regime responded to the demonstrations with violent repression, unleashing a civil war. In contrast to Tunisia and Egypt, Western powers were quick to get involved, deploying NATO bombing raids that laid waste to much of the country. The regime fell and Gaddafi was killed by rebel forces in August, but this was no longer the revolution many had dreamt of. Libya was broken.

Ordinary Libyans, determined to rebuild their shattered lives, continued to sing the song:

> We will remain here,
> Until the pain is gone,
> We will live here,
> Until life is sweet.

According to the BBC's North Africa correspondent Rana Jawad, 'Sawfa Nabqa Huna' was everywhere in Libya: 'It was coming out of every car that passed by, in every house that you visited and every shop you went in to.' It also travelled across the region. Versions recorded in Lebanon and Egypt captured the hearts of audiences who related to the themes of pain, pride and determination. A few years later it was also heard in far-off Dresden, Germany, sung by a choir composed of locals and recent refugees to the city. As choir member Samira explained:

> We changed the meaning of the song Sawfa Nabqa Huna a little bit. It did mean we stay here in our home country before. And now we changed it a little bit to: We got to stay here in Dresden – in our town – even if there are racism movements who want to push the refugees out. We are saying, as a choir, we are staying here and we want to try to develop our town and to make it a better place.[1]

The fall of Mubarak in Egypt also inspired a popular uprising in Syria against the ruling dynasty of Bashar al-Assad. One of the regime's first reactions was to try to calm the situation and bolster support by playing patriotic songs in public places. For many years, the Syrian music industry had been closely aligned with the political establishment. Songs and chants of rebellion tended to come from those outside it. One of the most significant was written by a firefighter and part-time poet from Hama called Ibrahim al-Qashoush. An electrifying performance of the song can be found online, filmed on a phone in Hama town square on 27 June 2011. A vast, jubilant crowd fills the square cheering every lyric issued by the full-voiced firefighter. The song is based on traditional Levantine call-and-response folk forms – perfect for asserting political demands. The powerful rhythmic chant pivots urgently on a semitone before a short descending melody at the end of each line creates an infectious hook, compelling the crowd to join in and repeat the refrain 'Get out Bashar'.

> Your legitimacy here has ended – get out Bashar!
> Bashar you're a liar. To hell with you and your speech.
> Freedom is at the door. Time to leave Bashar. Get out Bashar!
> Maher you're a coward. You're the agent of the US.
> The Syrians won't be humiliated. Get out Bashar!
> Bashar you're an ass. And all those who support you. Get out Bashar!

The lines repeat and the excitement and intensity builds. Finally, Qashoush modulates up a tone – a powerful and uplifting musical moment to accompany the assertion 'We will remove Bashar with our strength. Syria wants freedom'. It remains one of the most remarkable pieces of revolutionary music to emerge from the brief Arab Spring. A few days later, the regime responded. On the 4 July 2011, Qashoush's dead body washed up on the shore of the Orontes River. His throat had been slit and voice-box ripped out.

The story of the music of the Arab revolutions is important. Musicians are seldom on the frontline of the struggles that change the world. Although their songs sometimes later become emblematic of important struggles, they are usually based on second-hand accounts. Even the most politically engaged musicians usually take time to translate their experiences into good music. As Leon Trotsky once explained:

The heart of the matter is that artistic creativity, by its very nature, lags behind the other modes of expression of a man's spirit, and still more of the spirit of a class. It is one thing to understand something and express it logically, and quite another thing to assimilate it organically, reconstructing the whole system of one's feelings, and to find a new kind of artistic expression for this new entity. The latter process is more organic, slower, more difficult to subject to conscious influence

– and in the end it will always lag behind. The political writing of a class hastens ahead on stilts, while its artistic creativity hobbles along on crutches.[2]

Trotsky's observation has often proved accurate. Music can't always keep pace with events. Beethoven's famous retraction of the dedication of his third symphony to Napoleon Bonaparte is a good example. By the time the symphony was complete, Napoleon had betrayed the revolution by declaring himself emperor. No doubt, it was not the last time a disillusioned composer has furiously scribbled out the name at the top of a manuscript. But what the Arab revolutions showed is that occasionally, far from hobbling behind events, musicians are central to critical moments of mass struggle. They tend to be unsigned, amateur musicians and their songs are communicated directly to the people via megaphones, PA systems or the internet – unmediated by the traditional gatekeepers of the music industry or mainstream media. They do far more than simply provide a soundtrack for 'the festival of the oppressed' as Lenin once described revolutions. Their songs can also capture and define the spirit of a growing movement, giving courage to long oppressed people and uniting them around a set of demands. In the short-lived Arab Spring, musicians were among the first to people the barricades – or occupy the squares – and among the last to leave. Many have paid a high price for their bravery.

CHAPTER ELEVEN

Rebel Music Manifesto

So, what is to be done? What can we do to make sure that culture serves the interests of the many rather than the few? How can music help change the world for the better? I certainly don't have all the answers, but if I've persuaded you that the questions are important, then in a sense my work here is done. But still, I'd like to offer a few thoughts . . .

Community Music

In a residential area, a few paces from the centre of Brixton in south London, stands an old Georgian public house called the Effra Hall Tavern. Beneath the building, the river Effra, from which it takes its name, slips away unseen. Inside, beer and Jamaican rum flow, keeping locals lubricated. It's Thursday night, the football has ended, and the big screens scroll away while the band unzip instrument cases and greet friends in the bustling, growing crowd. Within a few minutes, the joint is jumping. Guitarist Alan Weekes leads the eight-piece band through a joyous set of muscular jazz, down dirty blues and old-school ska and reggae. There is no stage, and by the second set the small space between the musicians is filled with gyrating bodies. Sharp-suited Caribbean pensioners spin young blondes; ageing rude boys and bearded hipsters nod along approvingly, and a twinkly-eyed, gold-toothed, red bowler-hatted dandy – known to locals as 'The Chemist' – performs bizarre cock-leg dance moves, physically impossible to most men half his age, while hollering words of advice to the band. This is a night where the whole community meets, dances, drinks and occasionally falls in love. Music is the catalyst for the communal creation of an atmosphere that noisily, but without fanfare, washes away prejudices and fears and brings out the best in people.

Such nights never feature in music magazine editorials, anthologies of protest music, or rock 'n' roll halls of fame. But their value to people around the world is immeasurable. This is music as centrepiece and cement of community. It's worth considering what makes it effective in that role. Admission is free and there are no dress codes or restrictions beyond licensing laws on who can be there. Sure enough a mixed crowd reflecting the diverse local population show up. The absence of a stage feels significant. With no physical separation between band and audience, other codes that usually separate us start to dissolve too. At big gigs we buy tickets, pay booking fees, queue, are searched by security, herded in and sold over-priced drinks in plastic cups. They can feel more akin to a budget airline flight than a night of creative stimulation. We're separated from the band by barriers, bouncers and photographer pits and performers use every theatrical trick to emphasise how different they are from the audience – elaborate costumes, huge lighting rigs and clever music sequencing technology to beef up the sound. But here at the Effra, the implicit message is that we are all equals who respect and look out for each other. The musicians make no pretensions to stardom. They are not celebrities to be 'followed' on social media or anywhere else. They simply offer up their music – raw, direct and for the most part un-amplified – and the music is great. This is culture treating us as adults, as participants in a community, as trustworthy citizens – rather than cash cows to be herded around and milked dry. When people are treated well, they respond accordingly.

To be clear, I'm not suggesting that big music events are all bad. They can offer an exhilarating sense of connectedness, and at their best, a life-changing source of inspiration. Political activists certainly shouldn't turn their backs on them – the more we can influence the branding of big events and find ways to present our politics at them the better. But if we want to erode the alienation we experience in our everyday lives, we must build trust, confidence and solidarity in our communities. We must get to know our neighbours. There are few better places for that to begin than on an impromptu dance-floor in a pub, park, street or tenement block. Thursday night at the Effra is just one of countless examples of music playing this role – of creating this communal space. Every type of music event from hip-hop bloc parties to village choirs in church halls help bring people together as active participants in their culture. The genre doesn't matter and the music doesn't have to be live. What matters is that people collectively make the event and feel a sense of ownership. The more we experience how satisfying collective ownership of a cultural event can feel, the more confidence we might find to explore the possibility that collective ownership might work for other parts of our lives. If we can make a great party without celebrities, branding, a corporate infrastructure, security and the rest, perhaps we can make other things that way too.

Music For Us By Us (All)

If music can help foster solidarity and shape our communities, we should ensure everyone has access to it. Culture is too important to be left to cultural workers, professional musicians and so on . . . Sidney Finkelstein wrote the following words about jazz in 1948. They remain an excellent manifesto for all music:

Jazz reasserts the fact that music is something that people do, as well as listen to; that art is not limited to a specialised profession, but should be in the possession of everybody. It restores the 'amateur' creation that must be part of every culture if it is to be a healthy one. It restores creative music and musical creation to the people. It proclaims that music is one of the means through which people live as well as make a living. It reveals how deep are the desire and the love for making music among people, and how great are their resources. It proves, not that elaborate technique and knowledge are unimportant, for they are, but that they are not essential; that if people can get or make any musical instruments, they will learn how to handle them, and if they have no instruments, they will use their voices; that music is a language of human communication, and that people, if given any opportunity, will always make of it something that becomes great art, for it contains living emotion, the felt presence of a human being.[1]

Significant barriers remain to any semblance of democratic participation in culture: unequal access to resources, long hours worked by low-paid workers, inadequate childcare provision, sexism and racial prejudice, to name a few. Such barriers must be dismantled. At the moment there is a real risk that more, not fewer, barriers will blight culture. Schemes set up to increase diversity in the arts are facing devastating funding cuts which threaten to roll back many of the advances made over the last few decades.

Wherever we work and play we must do whatever we can to stamp out every injustice and prejudice that prevents people from making and enjoying music. We must defend schemes that help poorer and marginalised communities to access music and should think creatively and ambitiously about new schemes to perform that role. To guarantee that young people have role models and opportunities, we should demand quota systems to ensure equal numbers of female artists on radio playlists and festival line ups. Over time and with proper planning and support such quotas could be rolled out to include crew, front-of-house staff, studio engineers, radio producers, A&R people, record company executives and every other role. Quotas could also help ensure that black and minority ethnic people are properly represented. Music is a powerful part of a cultural conversation that changes our world. Anyone with a shred of concern for real democracy must fight to ensure that all voices can join that conversation and be heard.

Make Good Music

When asked what type of music they like, a thoughtful music lover may well reply *good music*. Good and bad exist within every genre and it's rewarding to keep your ears open for the good examples of each and every style. But what is it that makes music good? The question could be the sole subject of far longer books, but it's still worth considering a few ideas. In his 1959 book *The Necessity of Art*, Ernst Fischer identified three things we should avoid:

1. 'Self-complacent virtuosity which exists for its own sake, that is to say virtuosity not concerned with solving structural problems in music but only in technical brilliance, with bravura, with stunning the audience.'
2. 'Crass imitation, slavish repetition of old canons, cloying harmony and sweetness in a world of dissonances, romantic pastoral tunes designed to muffle the roar of jet bombers overhead.'
3. 'The forcible removal of all warmth and feeling. Necessary as it was after a period of hysterical effusiveness in music to carry out a cold-water cure, to get rid, as it were, of the surplus fat of music so as to reintroduce lost discipline and dignity, we cannot accept the principle that music has nothing to do with the expression of feeling but is only the embodiment of pure form.'

Similar thoughts were succinctly voiced by Sidney Finkelstein who also attempted to describe what makes music good: 'Good music asserts the presence within it of a living, thinking and feeling human being, exploring the world about him. Bad music attempts to satisfy the needs of the present by finding formulas in the past.'[2]

Good art doesn't try to dazzle with its own brilliance, distract us from reality or parrot accepted wisdom and formulas of the past. It dares to honestly communicate how the person making it feels about their experience of the world around them. When an artist does that successfully, their art will resonate and touch the lives of others. Honesty is key even – or perhaps especially – when times are hard and the message bleak. As Bertolt Brecht's poem 'Motto' asks:

In the dark times
Will there be singing?
Yes, there will also be singing
About the dark times.

Artistic honesty doesn't come easily in a world where culture and our sense of self have been bent out of shape by commercial concerns – a world in which young artists are all too often told they must imitate established acts and compete with one another. But it remains a goal we must work towards.

More often than painting, sculpture or literature, good music relies on successful collaboration. It is the result of people working together to express shared feelings, or at least several people skilfully interpreting and articulating the heartfelt perspective of an individual. Put simply, you need a good band. An analogy I've found useful when talking to music students is the band as a living organism.

When, for example, the brain sends a message to the legs to run, the heart and lungs respond accordingly, ensuring that enough oxygen is circulating the body to make it possible. So too will a rhythm section respond dynamically to musical choices made by a soloist, and a band as a whole, to the nuances of a singer's performance.

The analogy has its limitations. For budding musicians, that desire and ability to respond doesn't always come naturally. It requires some planning, practise and effort. At its core is good communication between musicians, and communication relies on the ability to hear, and a commitment to listen to one another. The first part – the ability to hear – is largely a technical issue. It involves positioning of amplifiers and relative sound levels. If one instrument is drowning others out, it needs to be turned down, and so on. The second part – a commitment to listen – is both a decision each individual needs to make and a skill that must then be developed. Acquiring that skill requires on-going personal effort. How successfully each musician does so will affect everyone in the band.

The qualities that make a band good are some of the same qualities in microcosm that make for good human relations in general. Hearing; listening; good communication; honesty . . . The template for making good music helps us think about the qualities that make society as a whole better. Can you hear each of the voices that make up your community? Are you listening?

Don't Be Scared of Politics

If good music doesn't come easily, good explicitly political music can be even harder to get right. But hard is neither impossible nor undesirable. Those of us who want to change the world and happen to be musicians should give it a go. We need to consider how we can use music to open minds and give confidence to people in our communities and political movements. The mission goes beyond composing music and writing lyrics. It must encompass a re-evaluation of the totality of our experience of music: media, marketing, events, education and so on.

We must have no truck with those who argue that music and politics don't mix. At best, their definition of politics is too narrow. Most likely they simply aren't courageous enough to admit, even to themselves, that they have no desire to change the world. To argue that 'politics should be left to the politicians' is to argue for things to remain as they are. As Ernst Fischer asserts:

Society needs the artist and it has the right to demand of him that he should be conscious of his social function. This right was never doubted in any rising, as opposed to decaying, society. It was the ambition of the artist full of the ideas and experiences of his time not only to represent reality but to shape it.[3]

Anyone who wants to shape reality, to change the world, needs first to answer two questions. One was famously posed by Marvin Gaye and the other by Lenin: 'What's Going On?' and 'What Is To Be Done?' Music that carefully and honestly addresses either question can be very valuable. Too many pop songs confine the answer to the first question to matters of the heart. Certainly we need love songs, songs about the pain of unrequited love, songs of separation, and so on. But we also need songs about the world beyond romantic love ... songs that share our experience of work, the state of our communities and stories from people's histories. The Marvin Gaye song that poses the question is one such example. Billie Holiday's 'Strange Fruit', Dolly Parton's 'Nine to Five', the Specials' 'Ghost Town', Plan B's 'Ill Manors', Janelle Monáe's 'Hell You Talmbout' and Kendrick Lamar's 'Alright' are others. Songs that address the second question can be harder to write – or at least easier for others to criticise. But that's no reason for songwriters to abstain from making directly political demands with their music. Whether or not people agree, you will at least start a discussion. The Austrian composer Olga Neuwirth made the case in her address to a mass demonstration against Austria's fascist coalition government in 2000:

> For me as a composer, the meaning of music can't be a matter of soothing people and making them compliant by promising a communal spirit that crosses

all frontiers . . . I would like my listeners to be people who consciously think things over, who think for themselves, who regard music and art as a whole as a mirror of human searching, of people who want to grasp how things are, to cast off impositions, and to leap into the unknown . . . .[4]

Of course, not all music can or should be overtly political. Even the most committed political musicians have understood this. Woody Guthrie didn't just write songs in opposition to fascism and the bosses, he also penned nonsensical ditties for children and whimsical songs of love and lust. We need ambiguity in art, room for interpretation; music that invites a conversation about its meaning rather than delivers a line. But even when music isn't directly political, we can still engage in the battle for context – for the perceived values of the musicians who create it. This important project takes many forms. Historical accounts reminding us of the radical roots shared by canonised figures such as Beethoven, Mozart, Coltrane, Holiday and Sinatra are one important part of that. Campaigns inviting musicians to sign up and show their support are another.

Earlier, we looked at the inspiring achievements of Rock Against Racism. Its contemporary equivalent, Love Music Hate Racism – a similar grassroots and trade-union backed initiative – has successfully staged gigs across Britain including a free carnival attended by

80,000 people in East London's Victoria Park on the 30th anniversary of the Rock Against Racism carnival held in the same place. This was when the far-right were again threatening to make an electoral breakthrough in the area. The RAR/LMHR model has spawned numerous other successful music-led campaigns against other forms of prejudice. The branding of the AFROPUNK festivals, which promote new black music on both sides of the Atlantic, reflect a growing awareness of the inter-sectional nature of oppression. At a recent London event, artists from Lady Leshurr to Young Fathers and Grace Jones performed beneath a huge banner stating:

NO SEXISM
NO RACISM
NO ABLEISM
NO AGEISM
NO HOMOPHOBIA
NO FATPHOBIA
NO TRANSPHOBIA
NO HATEFULNESS

With no mention of poverty or class it's lacking as a political manifesto. But it's an excellent code of conduct. We must keep up this good work. The tactic of cultural boycott discussed earlier is another important example of the sorts of initiatives we can use to regain control of our culture and raise the level of political debate.

The desire by rulers to co-opt culture for their own economic and political agenda is a theme discussed throughout this book. Overtly political songs and campaigns make that process far more difficult. They can help to amplify good sense at times when rulers and the mass media are peddling division, distraction or war.

Be Creative With Places and Spaces

It could have been the enigmatic street artist Banksy who wrote the following prophetic lines:

> I want paintings to be connected not by cords but by their artistic significance to walls ... to the purpose of a building, to the character of a room ... and not hanging like a hat on a hat stand. Picture galleries, those concentration camps for colours and beauty, serve but as a monstrous appendage to our colourless and unsightly daily reality.[5]

In fact, they were penned by Leon Trotsky in 1908. In the same way that Banksy has popularised political and satirical art by taking his stencils to the streets, musicians too must be creative with context. We must continue to break beyond the officially sanctioned venues, airwaves and festivals. I say 'continue' because the history of music has always in part been a history of unsanctioned social get-togethers. Carnival is perhaps the most important example, but not the only one. From troubadours in the market places of medieval Europe to London's underground grime scene, people have always partied wherever they can. Often the choice of venue is a pragmatic one made by people without means. Conflict with the authorities only arises when such gatherings attract unwanted attention.

But sometimes the choice of venue is deliberately provocative. It was the locations and presentation of Pussy Riot's performances, rather than the musical content, that propelled them onto the world's media, and into prison. On 21 February 2012, five members of the group attempted a performance of their 'Punk Prayer – Mother of God, Chase Putin Away!' in Moscow's Cathedral of Christ the Saviour. The band was protesting against the Russian Orthodox Church's support for President Putin's election campaign. Church security stopped the band after just 40 seconds, but a video of the performance posted on social media attracted huge attention.

Brave and inspiring as they may be, it's important to acknowledge the inherent elitism of such stunts. They have to be secretive acts planned and executed by a small number of dedicated activists. As such, the degree to which they contribute to the building of a movement capable of changing the world is debatable. Nevertheless, Pussy Riot deserves our solidarity. Their approach teaches us all to be creative and bold – to keep finding fresh ways of challenging the powerful, and starting a debate. The idea of combining theatrical costumes and live music to political effect was also seized by Ukraine's Dakh Daughters, who performed at the Maidan Square anti-government protests of December 2013. As their name suggests – like Pussy Riot – they are also all-female. These are welcome developments we should encourage and learn from.

Where people have already successfully reclaimed public space, we need to remain vigilant. Carnival, Pride, love parades and summer festivals are constantly politically contested. Authorities will try to restrict, sanitise and depoliticise such events, partly to attract lucrative corporate sponsorship. We need to bring the politics back. An interesting initiative launched by some of the organisers of the Trinidad carnival is a now annual theatrical re-enactment by local students and volunteers of the Canboulay riot of 1881, mentioned earlier in this book. Another is the Left Field stage at the Glastonbury festival, Rebel Soul at Shambala and other festival spaces dedicated to overtly political music and debate. These are creative and practical ways to remind people about the politics behind the party and to encourage engagement in struggles now. We need more initiatives like them.

Be Smart With Social Media

We also need to be creative and clever in our use of social media. In hindsight, my campaign song 'Freedom for

Palestine' may have been considerably more successful if I'd consulted the man responsible for getting Rage Against The Machine (RATM) to Christmas number one in the UK chart of 2009 – fellow Essex man Jon Morter. Fed up with the chart dominance of Simon Cowell's TV show *The X Factor*, whose winners had occupied the prestigious seasonal slot for several years, Morter enlisted the help of his then wife Tracy and started his campaign.

The political premise was far softer than mine and it centred around a song, 'Killing in the Name', that was already known and loved by millions. But Morter deserves credit for cunning, guile, punk-rock irreverence, depth of knowledge and tenacity that leaves the 'Freedom for Palestine' campaign team in the dust. Initially, to gain an audience, Morter exploited loopholes in Facebook enabling him to nab the 'administrator' status of several existing Facebook groups. He then cleverly fed the media half-truths and rumours of scandal to make the campaign newsworthy. Days before the critical chart week, Simon Cowell reacted angrily to a question about the campaign, labelling it 'cynical' and 'stupid'. His reaction went viral propelling the story onto the front page of the *Daily Mirror*. Morter didn't rest on his laurels, but instead used every possible trick to keep the momentum going until the chart closed. Hours after Rage's top spot was announced, Cowell played his ruling class role to perfection, phoning Morter to apologise for his previous remarks and to offer him a very well paid job . . . if you can't beat it, co-opt it. Morter declined the offer.

He went on to help the campaign to save the much-loved BBC radio station 6 Music; joined the marketing team responsible for securing the top spot for the Rolling Stones' *Exile on Main St*, and, in what was arguably the most politically significant of his chart campaigns, also helped to secure a Christmas number one for the Justice Collective's version of 'He Ain't Heavy, He's My Brother' in 2012. The record attempted to draw attention to the campaign started by families affected by the Hillsborough Stadium disaster of April 1989, in which 96 Liverpool football fans were crushed to death. Police culpability for the incident was covered up and instead the victims were smeared by police chiefs, senior Tory politicians and the *Sun* newspaper. The Justice Collective's chart success received far less publicity than RATM had three years before, but still, it remains an important example of popular culture being used to shine a light on injustice. Campaigners' efforts were finally rewarded in April 2016, when an inquest concluded the supporters had been unlawfully killed due to grossly negligent failures by police and ambulance services.

In a list that can usefully be applied to all types of political activism, Morter summarises his strategy as:

- Gain the troops and keep them: Get your network excited by the vision of a victory, while stressing that it can only be achieved by working together.
- Make your voice heard somehow: Be creative and bold and don't play by the rules. Well behaved people don't make history.
- Don't be afraid of making mistakes: Try things out – don't worry if they don't work. Mistakes are fine, as long as you learn from them.
- Clear Communication: Having got people's attention, tell them clearly what you want them to do.

Get Yourself Connected

Music best contributes to progressive political change when it arises from a broader movement. As Sidney Finkelstein put it: 'The composer's own psychology, as well as his understanding of others, is shaped by the role he plays in relation to the great social movements of his time, that affect him in company with all others.'[6]

Musicians should seek to strengthen demonstrations, strikes and other forms of struggle – not compete with them. In July 2005, around a quarter of a million protestors gathered in Edinburgh, where G8 leaders were meeting, with the demand 'Make Poverty History'. Bob Geldof promptly organised a Live 8 gig up the road at Murrayfield Stadium. It's a moot point whether the gig contributed to the protests or pulled people away from them and towards a softer political tone. Inevitably, one invited celebrity was the multi-millionaire U2 frontman Bono, causing sceptical satirists to produce a run of 'Make Bono History' T-shirts. I was performing at the gig with 1 Giant Leap and took the opportunity to meet Geldof. I asked him why he had been pictured in the newspapers that week cosying up to the warmongering then Prime Minister, Tony Blair. He defiantly replied 'because I like him', before I was physically bundled away by thuggish security.

If a gig is timetabled to clash with demonstrations called nearby, we need to be at the demonstrations. The essence of Gil Scott-Heron's classic song 'The Revolution Will Not Be Televised' remains true: it's not enough to spectate or sing from the sidelines. We must join those on the streets, occupying workplaces, and so on. We must feed our creativity with our experiences of political struggle and vice-versa. My contention throughout this book is that culture matters – more than many people realise. But it does not change the world on its own. The more removed an artist is from other sites of political struggle, the less relevant their artistic output will be. In the words of the Stereo MC's, 'Get yourself connected'. Get involved with campaigns locally, nationally and globally. Join a relevant trade union – and then fight for it to be more politically ambitious and proactive. See whether any political parties make sense to you – if one does sign up. Speak to the people you work with and meet on your travels about the issues that concern you. Listen with an open mind, and learn from what they have to say. Build lasting relationships with other campaigners. And make music.

CHAPTER TWELVE

Conclusion

It's a beautiful spring day in central London and a quarter of a million people are marching through the streets of the city. All ages, ethnicities and every corner of the country are represented. They are here to demand an end to the Tory government's policy of 'austerity' – a series of cuts to the welfare state, public sector wages, pensions and living conditions for many poor and middle income Britons. My job at the demo is to DJ as the sea of people enters Parliament Square. I've lined up some Damian Marley, Ana Tijoux, Kendrick Lamar, Kate Tempest, Janelle Monáe, Captain Ska and Young Fathers to name a few. Anyone who tells you there's no new rebel music simply doesn't have their ears to the ground. Some of the classics are as relevant as ever too – Joni Mitchell's 'Big Yellow Taxi' and Grandmaster Flash and the Furious Five's 'The Message' go down a storm. And, incidentally, it is a singer, Charlotte Church, who gets all the press attention and makes the most rousing speech that afternoon:

We need to win back young minds and save ourselves from decades of yuppie rule. The way we do that is with fresh ideas, positive messages, new theories, engaging art and more public figures sticking their head above the parapet . . . There is only one way to fight the onslaught of crusading austerity and that is to come together in unity . . . we will not be silenced.

With the sound of police helicopters above me and Max Romeo's 'War Ina Babylon' reverberating up Whitehall, I reflect on everything I've learned about this love and vocation of mine . . .

Since the dawn of humankind, music has reflected and helped shape the conditions of our existence. Its story traces our changing relationship with nature and each other. Music emerged from our intimate connection with the natural world. It accompanied communal tasks such as washing clothes in rivers and was later played on the adapted tools of hunting and agriculture. When human society started to divide into classes, music divided with it. Different types of music reflected the experiences of the different classes who made or paid for it. Music also bolstered their competing agendas in the class struggles that have shaped history. Economic dynamism has often spurred technological innovation, which in turn alters the sound and impact of music. Advances in metallurgy, print setting, wax recordings, the phonograph, metallic tape and digital technology are all key examples. The impact of each was mediated by the outcome of broader social struggles. Musicians have responded to every such struggle and all the convulsions of world history.

Some have paid a high price for challenging the status quo, while others have been richly rewarded for defending it. The most popular songs of recent decades suggest that feelings of alienation – a creeping sense of loneliness or dislocation from nature and each other – are widely experienced in the modern world. It seems that music, an artistic form born of our intimacy with nature, increasingly reflects and often laments how estranged that relationship has become.

So, where are things heading? Well, new technology continues to change music, the music industry, and our relationship with both. With the touch of a tablet, we can now access almost anything. Most of us need help navigating the vast new oceans of online content – the role of the DJ/selector/curator has in some senses never been more important. Without them, it's easy to feel bewildered by choice; overfed yet undernourished. But with the right help, greater choice can inspire curiosity and creativity. Sure enough, we've seen a proliferation of diverse new scenes. Many orbit musical styles from bygone days. Pitch up to the Cable Cafe Bar on Brixton Road any Tuesday night and you'll find 1930s hot-club swing sounding authentic and looking fresh faced, for example. This is music reclaimed from the dusty archives of the Culture Industry and given new life by everyday enthusiasts. We should welcome such developments.

As well as offering increased access to existing music, new technology also facilitates and shapes the creation of new music – music that reflects our experience of this fast-changing world. In countries like Britain, countless young people who can't afford a beer at the local pub will instead stay home making tunes in their bedrooms on basic computers before sharing them on social media. Much of the music will be derivative and dull – pre-programmed loops lazily thrown together. But some of it will be completely original and heartfelt responses to the lived experiences of its composers. As long as human beings have a future, new forms of music will evolve.

Meanwhile, the mainstream music industry faces challenges. An increasingly unstable world economy; attempts by some artists to sell directly to their fans; and a new generation who expect to download music for free, to name a few. Endless industry magazine editorials and conference keynotes have wrestled with the issues – establishment figures clearly fear the potential threat to their dominance and revenue. But we shouldn't confuse the health of the mainstream music industry with that of music itself. Steve Albini (producer of Nirvana, the Pixies, P.J. Harvey and countless others) is optimistic. In a recent talk, he brilliantly deconstructed the commonly uttered platitude: 'We need to figure out how to make this digital distribution work for everyone.'

So, who is this 'we'? The administrative parts of the
old record business, that's who. The vertical labels
who hold copyright on a lot of music. They want to
do the figuring. They want to set the agenda. And they
want to do all the structural tinkering. The bands, the
audience, the people who make music and who pay for
it – they are conspicuously not in the discussion.[1]

In his upbeat assessment of the impact of new
technology, Albini described the very tangible ways
in which bands and audiences can now converge and
commune without being chaperoned by the old industry
profiteers. Due to the internet, Albini's own relatively
unknown band has arranged successful club tours of
far-flung lands. He's met delighted fans, made new
friends and come home with a few bucks in his pocket,
all without a record label. He concludes:

So there's no reason to insist that other obsolete
bureaux and offices of the lapsed era be brought along
into the new one. The music industry has shrunk. In
shrinking it has rung out the middle, leaving the bands
and the audiences to work out their relationship from
the ends. I see this as both healthy and exciting. If
we've learned anything over the past 30 years, it's that
left to their own devices bands and their audiences can
get along fine: the bands can figure out how to get their

music out in front of an audience and the audience will figure out how to reward them.[2]

Not everyone shares Albini's optimism. Thom Yorke, David Byrne and Billy Bragg have all joined a chorus of voices warning that artists are the ones being squeezed as old revenue streams run dry. The old captains of the culture industries are now the owners of the new digital platforms and the percentage of profits they pass on to artists is slimmer than ever. Corporate capitalism has a knack for seizing clever innovations and making them its own. But Albini is right to imply that it doesn't have to be this way. The principle that the people who make things and the people who use those things can 'figure things out' – without the profiteers in the middle – is the essence of an exciting vision of a possible future.

At the moment, the production and consumption of everything from eggs to education is shaped by the logic of 'the market' – the premise that the enterprise has to make investors richer. Effectively, we live under a shareholder dictatorship and by definition their only concern is profit. If it's more profitable to force people into poverty or pollute the planet that is what will happen. In theory, elected governments should mediate shareholder's demands and keep the influence of capital in check. In reality, pretty much all have joined a humiliating limbo dance – competing to bend to demands for less regulation. Governments boast of moving from 'red tape to red carpets' in their clamour to prove they are the most investor friendly. When challenged about the logic of this race to the bottom they repeat the mantra that There Is No Alternative. But there could be. Workplaces could be owned and democratically controlled by the people who work in them and the communities they serve. Decisions about what we make, and how we make and distribute it could be based on people's needs. In short, capitalism could be replaced with a more democratic and equitable system. Community music schemes, carnivals, festivals, tours and music education would no longer have to rely on crumbs of sponsorship tossed from the corporate table. With societies' wealth rebalanced, there would be plenty to go around.

Ordinary people who currently spend all their time trying to make ends meet could finally start to express themselves creatively. The 'muck of ages' that corporate culture reinforces could be flushed away. Access to all types of music could be extended to everyone who's interested – no longer would prejudice or poverty get in the way of participation. Culture would be set free. We might finally arrive at Finkelstein's vision of:

> . . . a time when the artificial distinction between 'classical' and 'popular' will disappear; when music will take on different and varied forms, forms of song and dance and forms of powerful drama or psychological complexity. But all forms will be equally accessible

to people, and the only question to be asked will be, is it good or bad? Is it honest or dishonest? Does it give us pleasure to know it? Does it help us to know better our fellow human beings and the world which we share with them?[3]

Of course, those who think they have the most to lose will oppose such change. As we have seen, music is one weapon they deploy to help protect their privilege. Occasionally, it's also a means by which they set out their vision for the future. On 9 September 2014, the bigwigs at Apple Inc added U2's new album *Songs of Innocence* to the music collections of every one of the more than 500 million iTunes customers around the world, without the customers' consent. The stunt was, on the whole, badly received. It was largely seen to be an egotistical display of power – an act of cultural carpet bombing designed not only to grab headlines, but also to make the album so ubiquitous that revenue from radio play, syncs and tours was bound to follow. The flimsy defence was generosity – this was simply a gift that could easily be deleted if unwanted. But for many, the stunt left a bitter taste. As spam goes, a U2 album is innocuous enough, but the symbolism is chilling. It revealed a growing convergence of power away from ordinary people and towards a tiny, unaccountable global cabal with Orwellian powers to monitor and intervene in our lives.

Throughout this book we have looked at examples of rulers attempting to erode democracy. From bloody coups to the covert manipulation of culture, those with money have used every tactic available to get their way, regardless of what the rest of us think. Now they don't even let us choose our own music collection. More seriously, their rapacious desire to accumulate ever more profit is marching the world towards environmental catastrophe. We must stop them.

Those of us who love music have a role to play. We need to be aware of the various ways that rulers co-opt and use music to reflect and reinforce their values and push through their agenda. We must reject the idea that this use of music – this relationship between music and power – is natural or inevitable. Wherever possible we should expose and challenge it.

We also need to take concrete steps towards securing music as a tool for social progress – one that contributes to the building of a mass movement capable of changing the world. Music must come from and help strengthen our communities. We must defend local venues, organise events and encourage everyone to take part in creating culture. We must improve and expand music education and dismantle any and every barrier to participation – financial, physical, ideological, or otherwise. We must endeavour to make good music – music that is honest and heartfelt. We mustn't shy away from making music that is overtly political – music that raises important issues and provokes debate. We must encourage artists to publicly participate in progressive campaigns. Occasionally, this will mean observing boycotts. We must always strive to be creative, both in our music and our activism. Finally, we need to work together in co-ordinated, effective ways – we must get organised. Digital technology and social media can help with all these tasks, but we must make sure it's used to help facilitate rather than replace physical get-togethers.

From and for communities, or from and for corporations . . . The different visions for music point towards two different visions for humankind. The first is a vision of greater democracy – a world in which the dictates of the market are cast off and ordinary people figure things out collectively. The second, a vision of greater tyranny and continued exploitation of people and planet. Hope or denial. Socialism or barbarism.

Which path we take will be determined by our collective actions. The choice is ours. Those of us who decide to join the struggle for a better world will need to use every tool and tactic at our disposal. Understanding culture and reclaiming music is only part of the puzzle, but an important part – one that will help to reveal the bigger picture and inspire hope.

There will be trouble ahead, so let's face the music, together.

One, Two, One-Two-Three-Four . . . .

Notes

Chapter Two

1. Plato's *Republic* book IV (Fowler translation).
2. S. Frith, *The Sociology of Rock*, 1978, p. 195.
3. D. Byrne, *How Music Works*, 2012, p. 135.
4. T. Adorno, *Prisms*, 1955, p. 149.
5. T. Adorno, *Aesthetic Theory*, 1970, 1984, p. 432.
6. Horkheimer and Adorno, *Dialectic of Enlightenment*, 1944, 1979, p. xiv.
7. R. Eley quoted in Cornelius Cardew, *Stockhausen Serves Imperialism*, 1974, p. 11.
8. *Ibid.*, p. 13.
9. A. Troitsky interviewed in Leslie Woodhead's documentary *How the Beatles Rocked the Kremlin*, 2009.
10. Troitsky in Woodhead, *How the Beatles Rocked the Kremlin*.
11. Francis Stonor Saunders, *Who Paid the Piper*, 1999, p. 2.
12. *Ibid.*, p. 48.
13. *Ibid.*, p. 50.
14. *Ibid.*, p. 291.

15. Felix Belair in the New York Times, 6 November 1955, quoted F. Kofsky, *Black Nationalism and the Revolution Music*, 1970, p. 109 footnote.
16. F. Kofsky, *Black Nationalism and the Revolution Music*, p. 110.
17. *Ibid.*, p. 110.

Chapter Three

1. J. Cowley, *Carnival, Canboulay and Calypso: Traditions in the Making*, 1996, p. 30.
2. *Ibid.*, p. 2.
3. C. Gilkes, Trinidad Carnival, Afri-Caribbean Resistance, Trinicentre.com, 23 February 2003.
4. L. Bradley, *Sounds Like London: 100 years of Black Music in the Capital*, 2013, p. 79.
5. Bradley, *Sounds Like London*, p. 82.

Chapter Four

1. Manthia Diawara quoted in M. Veal, *Fela: The Life and Time of an African Musical Icon*, 2000, p. 56.
2. J.W. Shipley, *Living the Hiplife*, 2013, p. 42.
3. *Daily Times* journalist quoted in Veal, *Fela*, p. 59.
4. F. Kuti interviewed in the 1980 film *Music is the Weapon*, 00:10.
5. M. Roach quoted in D. Margolick, *Strange Fruit*, 2000, p. 23.

6. S. Grafton quoted in Margolick *Strange Fruit*, p. 77.

7. A. Meeropol interviewed in 1971 and quoted in Margolick, *Strange Fruit*, p. 31.

8. L. Feather quoted in Margolick *Strange Fruit*, p. 63.

9. A. Ross, *The Rest is Noise*, 2007, p. 237.

10. *Ibid.*, p. 249.

11. *Ibid.*, p. 341.

12. B. Varga, *Conversations with Iannis Xenakis*, 1996, p. 47.

13. K. Stockhausen quoted in Ross, *The Rest is Noise*, p. 374.

14. T. Adorno quoted in Ross, *The Rest is Noise*, p. 388.

Chapter Five

1. P. Crossley-Holland, *The Pelican History of Music 1*, ed. A. Robertson and D. Stevens, 1960, p. 18.

2. *Ibid.*, p. 77.

3. S. Finkelstein, *The Artistic Expression of Alienation*, quoted in M. Solomon, *Marxism and Art*, 1979, p. 278.

4. BBC Four documentary, *The Richest Songs in the World*, presented by Mark Radcliffe, 2012.

5. Adorno and Eisler, *The Sociology of the Musician*, quoted in Solomon, *Marxism and Art*, p. 376.

6. Substance Abuse and Mental Health Services (US Government department) statistics for

18–64-year-olds employed full time 2008–12, reported in the *Independent*, 25 October 2015.

Chapter Six

1. Quoted in D. Lynskey, *33 Revolutions Per Minute*, 2010, p. 278.
2. J. Jara, *Victor*, 1993, p. 124.
3. Victor Jara quoted in Jara, *Victor*, p. 117.
4. Don Letts rapproject.tv interview, 2007, www.youtube.com/watch?v=SO49fsho M4I.
5. Red Saunders quoted in D. Rachel, *Walls Come Tumbling Down*, 2016.
6. D. Widgery, *Beating Time: Riot 'n' Race 'n' Rock 'n' Roll*, 1986, p. 56.
7. N. George, *The Death of Rhythm & Blues*, 1988, p. 193.
8. M. Thatcher in an interview for *Woman's Own* magazine, 23 September 1987, archived at www.margaretthatcher.org/document/106689.
9. L. Garcia, *An Alternate History of Sexuality in Club Culture*, 2014, www.residentadvisor.net/feature.aspx?1927
10. N. Rodgers, *Le Freak*, 2011, p. 116.
11. *Ibid.*, p. 154.
12. www.legislation.gov.uk/ukpga/1994/33/part/V/enacted.
13. Matthew Collin, *Pop Grenade*, 2015, p. 90.

Chapter Seven

1. C. Harman, *A People's History of the World*, 2008, p. 150.
2. Y. Menuhin and C.W. Davis, *The Music of Man*, 1979, p. 168.
3. *Letters of the Young Engels*, 1976.
4. E. Fischer, *The Necessity of Art*, 1963, p. 63.
5. Thomas Edison quoted in M. Hamilton, *In Search of the Blues, Black Voices, White Visions*, 2007, p. 30.
6. John Lennon quoted in Tariq Ali, *Street Fighting Years*, 2005, pp. 363, 367.
7. Senator Bernie Sanders quote deemed accurate by politifact.com's Molly Moorhead, 31 July 2012.
8. Oxfam Policy Report, 18 January 2016.

Chapter Eight

1. Lady Leshurr quoted in the *Guardian*, 20 April 2013.
2. Creative & Cultural Skill report quoted by Lara Baker in *Huffington Post*, 21 June 2013.
3. A. Dot speaking at the Women of the World festival, London, 12 March 2016.
4. The Sutton Trust figures reported in *The Economist*, 27 February 2016.
5. J. Blunt quoted in the *Guardian*, 19 January, 2015.
6. C. Bryant quoted in the *Guardian*, 19 January, 2015.
7. J.W. Shipley, *Living the Hiplife*, 2013, p. 18.

Chapter Nine

1. *B'Tselem* report, 29 December 2009, www.btselem.
   org/gaza_strip/20091227_a_year_to_castlead_
   operation.
2. 'Goldstone Report' of the United Nations Fact
   Finding Mission on the Gaza Conflict to the Human
   Rights Council, 29 September 2009, www2.ohchr.
   org/english/.
3. *One Family in Gaza* can be viewed at http://vimeo.
   com/18384109.
4. www.wallofsilence.org/.
5. JewishJournal.com, 25 April 2012.
6. Anne Karpf et al., eds, *A Time to Speak Out*:
   Independent Jewish Voices, 2008, p. viii.
7. www.engageonline.org.uk/blog/article.php?id=297.
8. Brian Eno's open letter published September 2016.
9. The advert and more information can be found
   at: www.southafricanartistsagainstapartheid.com/
   2011/07/legal-victory.html.

Chapter Ten

1. Quote from BBC Trending report, 'The Arab
   Revolution Song That Went Viral', 22 August 2016.
2. L. Trotsky, *Class and Art*, quoted in M. Solomon,
   Marxism and Art, 1979, p. 196.

Chapter Eleven

1. S. Finkelstein, *Jazz: A People's Music*, 1964, p. 27.
2. *Ibid.*, p. 10.
3. E. Fischer, *The Necessity of Art*, 1963, p. 58.
4. O. Neuwirth speech made 19 February 2000 in front of Vienne Staatsoper. Documented on olganeuwirth. com.
5. L. Trotsky, *Culture and Revolution in the Thought of Leon Trotsky*, 1999, pp. 67–8.
6. S. Finkelstein, *Composer and Nation*, 1959, p. 17.

Chapter Twelve

1. S. Albini, keynote address at the Face the Music conference, Melbourne 2014.
2. *Ibid.*
3. S. Finkelstein, *Jazz: A People's Music*, 1964, p. 29.

Index